AIR FAIR

AIR FAIR

ALICE FURLAUD'S DISPATCHES FROM PARIS

PEREGRINE SMITH BOOKS
SALT LAKE CITY

First edition

93 92 91 90 89   5 4 3 2 1

Portions of this book appeared in the
New York Times

Copyright © 1989 by Alice Furlaud

Published by Gibbs Smith, Publisher,
P.O. Box 667, Layton, Utah 84041

Manufactured in the United States of
America

Design by J. Scott Knudsen

Cover illustration by Carol Norby

**Library of Congress Cataloging-in-
Publication Data**

Furlaud, Alice, 1929-
    Air fair : Alice Furlaud's dispatches
from Paris.
        p. cm.
    ISBN 0-87905-304-6 :
    1. Paris (France)–Social life and
customs–20th century. 2. New
England–Social life and customs. I. All
things considered (Radio program) II. Title.
DC737.F87   1989
944'.36–dc20   89-6443
                                          CIP

The paper used in this publication meets
the minimum requirements of American
National Standard for Information
Sciences–permanence of paper for
Printed Library Materials, ANSI
Z39.48-1984 ∞

To my late father,
Frederic Cooke Nelson,
and to my most
enthusiastic listener —
my mother

ACKNOWLEDGMENTS

With thanks to Bryant Haliday, the Shakespearean and horror-film actor, whose out-of-the-blue first words to me after a thirty-year pause in our acquaintance were, "You're going to be on the radio." This idea had never before entered my head.

Thanks also to the people who first implemented the idea: Brad Spear, Jo Anne Wallace, Jo Ann Kawell and Paulette Kernis.

Thankful memories of Robert Siegel and Neal Conan, successive chiefs of NPR's London bureau, who on my R&R trips to London after months of work in nerve-jangling Paris, gave me comfort, advice, lunch, and instructions on putting batteries into my tape recorder.

And always thanks to le Colonel ("We-Are-Just-Good-Friends") Bèze.

CONTENTS

FOREWORD

A confession is necessary right here at the beginning.

There is no Alice Furlaud.

Those of us responsible for the creation of the "Furlaud" character at National Public Radio are ashamed to admit to this fraud, but it is true. It was an innocent prank at first, but I suppose Hitler said that when he invaded Poland. We simply didn't think of the repercussions at the time.

The need to create Furlaud arose from the paltry journalistic entrees available to us from overseas. In the course of putting together the daily news program "All Things Considered," we had far too many serious stories going on the air from abroad.

"Couldn't we get some silly stuff from our London bureau?" an editor wondered at a staff meeting one day many years ago.

"No, our reporter there is all Euromissiles and Thatcher health policy," another countered. "No way we're going to get him to do light features."

Suddenly it dawned on me. "France!" I exclaimed, bolting out of my chair. "France! No one will check France! We can just make the stuff up. You know, fiction!"

"You're crazy, Silverman," said my boss (and not for the first or last time).

"No, wait a minute, boss," said Willy, the senior foreign editor. "He might have something there. The *New York Times* makes up all their stuff from France."

"And so do *Time* and *Newsweek!*" I screamed. "It's wide open territory."

The boss pondered this for what seemed like an eternity, but was, in fact, a very long time. "Okay," he muttered, "we do it. Just one condition."

"What's that?" I asked.

"We create a totally unbelievable reporter to do the job."

I agreed. "Yes! A nom de microphone. Something playful. And something that hints at what we're up to."

And that's where Allie Furlaud—or Allez Furlough, as we first envisioned it—came from. "To go on vacation" from reality was our intent in the creation of the name.

Since that day, many years ago, we've all taken turns churning out fabricated tales of garlic-eating festivals, of outlandish museum openings, and of wealthy cat lovers, all gleefully sprinkled with improbably Gallic characters and charm. I imagine Furlaud to be a thin, grey-haired woman of ageless enthusiasm for life. She'd have to be full of good humor and braced with an endless supply of words. Furlaud, in fact, would be hard to shut up, but who would want to? She'd be forever eighteen years old, a woman of the world, yet surprised at each new encounter with humanity doing its thing. She'd collect and celebrate unique characters, and never be condescending, because she'd be the greatest character of all.

Incidentally, among the actresses who have portrayed Furlaud have been some of radio's finest stars, all of whom worked considerably below scale.

And now this book. Why put together a book to prolong the fraud? Well, frankly, they told us there was money in books, and we in public radio jump when we see dollar signs. But it was more than that: we wanted to preserve what we cast to the broadcast wind. For all the years we've worked in this business, no one has been able to convince those of us in the studio that anyone hears this stuff. But a book! A book you can carry down the street, leave in the car, wedge in the door.

I hope you enjoy our collective effort between these covers. It's been no easy task faking this stuff. I know that if there really were an Allie Furlaud, she'd appreciate you buying this book, and reading it, too.

ART SILVERMAN
Senior Producer
"All Things Considered"
April 1, 1989

INTRODUCTION

I learned how to do radio documentaries without meaning to, by discovering the BBC World Service on a tiny short-wave radio one year when I was living an isolated life on a Swiss mountain. All these wonderful people kept coming on the air—falling down in skating rinks; going up, with shaky voices, in balloons; peering into tunnels built under highways for toads. In an innocent, cheery way, they investigated all sorts of matters: a flea circus (don't inhale during a rehearsal or you'll swallow the whole cast), a ghost in an ancient pub, a toy fair for blind children. And just like the game little boys on that program, eagerly calling to each other, "Right! You turn this knob and it goes on," I found that you didn't need a picture in front of you to see deeply into things. No subject was too "visual" for these reporters: they showed you everything from the art of faking old masters to a butterfly sanctuary, without benefit of a television screen.

When I began, rather uncertainly at the age of fifty-one, to practice this art myself, I was constantly wounded to find that friends who heard my reports on the air had no idea of the frantic toil that went into them. A three-minute piece, they seemed to think, must have entailed three minutes' work. "Do you need a script to do those broadcasts?" or "I heard you the other night: was that live?" people would ask me—referring to the kind of little feature where my voice weaves in and out between the sounds of the mating call of a grey seal, a champagne tasting and Paris Mayor Jacques Chirac sharing his views with me in an atomic submarine.

I'm here to tell you, gentle listener, that when, on a news magazine program like "All Things Considered" or "Morning Edition," you hear the host or announcer say, "In strike-bound France, a new

1

group of malcontents has joined the striking can-can dancers, concierges and clairvoyants: the *éboueurs*, or street sweepers, have laid down their plastic twig brooms. Jane So and So reports," Jane herself has written those lines for the host. The next sounds you hear — angry shouts and chanting and police sirens — are not just wafted to you by magic, but were recorded by Jane out there in the crowd of demonstrators with her small, battered tape recorder, trying to shield her microphone from a lot of raging strikers who were bumping into her from all sides. But when her own voice comes in above the shrieks, saying, "One of ten thousand strikers on the protest march to the Bastille the other day was Jean-Paul Lefumier. He was there for a special reason: to burn his homemade effigy of Prime Minister Rocard," she will have written that description later, and have read it sitting in a small glass box, part of a sound studio bulging with the latest equipment imported from Japan, during which recording she may have received a loud and seriously ear-damaging tone sent by mistake through her headphones by the sound engineer. On the other hand, she may have read these lines into her own tape recorder, sitting in the bedroom of her attic apartment with the bedspread Scotch-taped over the window, pillows propped up around the tape recorder and the microphone strapped to a pile of books.

When Jean Lefumier comes on, saying, "For zees cow ze mud ees running een ze streets," his voice again has been taped by Jane, who has spent the morning looking for a striker who speaks English, followed him to the Bastille, taped what he has to say along with the opinions of sundry other demonstrators, recorded fifty or sixty seconds of chanting, honking and whatever else is going on,* and been swept along with the crowd all the way to the Gare de Lyon

---

*Taping this sound, or ambience, is the second-most embarrassing part of radio reporting (the most embarrassing is when you forget to turn on the tape recorder during an interview; I did this once with Margaux Hemingway but I didn't let on): you have to hold the microphone up for what seems ages, as if you were interviewing the air or a disembodied spirit. You have to ask the people around you to be quiet, even if moments before you have been begging them to say a few words. If you are interviewing a distinguished person on top of the Eiffel Tower, say, and you need the background sound of traffic from below, you even have to ask *him* to shut up and stand there for a full minute until the interview can be resumed. That's why reporters often get home and find they haven't got enough ambience to enrich their narrations.

before she can get over to the sidewalk. All this has swallowed up nearly a whole day. By the end of the week Jane has interviewed three other people about the strike, including, perhaps, Prime Minister Rocard's press secretary's first cousin (an appointment it will have taken a month or so to arrange). She has picked out from her cassettes the voices that best express both the facts and the emotions of the situation, also judging the tape for sound quality and intelligibility. She has written a story around these voices and sounds, using her stopwatch to keep it all down to around four and a half minutes.

She then has to go through an "edit," or the process of reading the whole thing over the telephone to whichever producer or editor has been assigned to her stories. If she's working for "All Things Considered," she has to call at exactly 3:00 P.M. Paris time, 9:00 A.M. Washington time. Otherwise she will miss her editor, who by 9:45 will be in the "morning meeting." If the editor is unavailable and doesn't call back (and it's amazing how often he doesn't), she has from 5:30 her time, when the meeting ends, till about 9:00 P.M., when everybody is concentrating on "All Things Considered" for the rest of the afternoon. During an hour or so of this time Jane's editor is out to lunch. While he is out to lunch, she is beginning to fade. By 7:30 she would love to have a cool glass of white wine, but she doesn't dare: she must be alert for the edit. And she has to have the edit before she can book a studio, get paid, go on to the next thing, etc.

This edit can be a breeze, or a sumo-wrestling match, with the reporter fighting for the survival of her story as she intended it. You have to read it to the Washington person confidently, playing all the roles and imitating the sounds. Some editors (like NPR's eagle-eared foreign editor, Cadi Simon, who knows what a franc sounds like going into a French pay telephone and accepts no substitutes) like to hear the "actualities" (voices and sounds), which means you have to unscrew the mouthpiece of the telephone and hook it up to your tape recorder with "alligator clips." I have not yet been required to do this—perhaps because people have learned what a technical moron I am.

Some editors are hard to sell ideas to, but behave like sweetie pies over the edit. Others will go for any old idea, but during the edit will shred the piece until it's unrecognizable. My husband, who has often sat wide-eyed while I have gone through this torment, says that, although the script may not have been improved by the edit, your own wits are sharpened in the cut and thrust of the duel. "That's a wonderful idea!" you say about some little change the editor wants early in the conversation. This may disarm him while you save your ammunition for the big change – when he wants to eliminate the whack of the guillotine slicing through a neck, for instance, and substitute a boring speech in the Assemblée Nationale. I will just add that editing with NPR is sissy stuff compared to editing with the Canadian Broadcasting people. They do it in a two- or three-way conference call – it has the effect of a firing squad.

After the script is approved, you have to do another kind of editing: cutting out the phrases in the actualities which slow the pace, are unintelligible, obscene, etc. If you are lucky and have a big tape recorder like a Revox or a Logix, on which you can transfer, or dub, the actualities from your cassettes to reel-to-reel tape, you can do the editing yourself. First you listen to locate the exact place you want to cut, by slowly moving the tape back and forth across the playback head. It's hard to recognize the words at first, because in this slow motion everybody's voice, even Catherine Deneuve's, groans like a dying sea elephant. You then mark the right place with a white grease pencil, slice out the part you don't want with a razor, and Scotch-tape the two cut ends back together. If it sounds all right after you've done this, you go on: otherwise you do the edit over again. (At this point you could tamper with the meaning somewhat, but listeners needn't worry: even if you were so dishonest as to contemplate this, you rarely have time.) You have to be sure to leave in the right breaths, which in the editing process sound like tidal waves, because it sounds odd to the listener if people don't breathe on the radio, even though the listener doesn't know why it sounds odd.

In the case of uncertain speakers of English, you often have to edit out endless "ers" and "ums" and shorten long hesitations, or snip out single words or phrases to put them in more intelligible places. During this process, you may lose the phrase – it's just a thin piece of plastic tape about as long as a hair ribbon. Even if you carefully hang it around your neck until it's needed, you can easily Scotch-tape it into the new place backwards. You can also amputate a finger if it gets in the way of a fast-forwarding reel.

I am terribly bad at all this, and anyway I have never been able to afford one of those machines. So my editing is done in a recording studio, which means spending an anxious hour or two hovering over a sound engineer (a French sound engineer; hovering over a time bomb would be more relaxing). After this, wrung with exhaustion, I have to go into the glass box and read the connecting narration, summoning all my "show-must-go-on" energy to sound sprightly and relaxed. Ordeals go on in these studios which make "voicing" the script a feat worthy of an Academy Award. There's heroism out here on these unsung battlegrounds!

The final stage — the mix — is the most fun, and if you use up all your studio time dubbing and editing, you will have to miss it. The mix is where the whole thing gets put together and the various bits of ambience you have recorded with such embarrassment out in the field are woven under the piece to give it the all-important atmosphere. Under ideal conditions you are in the studio when they play your recorded narration, ending, "Meanwhile, back at the Elysée Palace, President Mitterand was sadly sweeping his own sidewalk," and you get to signal to the engineer just where to add the slow swish-swish of the broom, which you have recorded days before with your zoom microphone, and just where to fade down the swishing as you sign off, "For National Public Radio, I'm Jane So and So in Paris. Swish-swish-swish . . ."

All this we far-flung free-lances do for roughly $250 to $350 a story. We grumble a lot about this, and sob to each other that the staff reporters back in Washington get free tapes, batteries and repairs; that they get sound technicians to record for them in the field, and that while our pieces and theirs have equal importance on the program, they do not get equal pay. But we rarely go back there and try to *be* staff reporters.

The one good thing to be said for our Spartan conditions is that they remind us of our unimportance, a precious quality most necessary to our work. We are *not* important. Our broadcasts are blown away like cobwebs, and any meaning or depth that lingers comes less from our words than the sounds we've recorded of the lonely hoot of an owl, the catch in a voice, a tolling cathedral bell or a chorus of students humming as a tear-gas bomb explodes nearby. It's the important, richly paid political journalists — as well as the politics into which they have such revered insights — which have gotten so completely out of hand. The other day Art Silverman, a star producer at NPR and the life and soul of the place, congratulated me on one of my rare political features: "Allie, why have you been writing about things like stray cats all these years when you could have been doing important stuff like this?" I told him I was thrilled at the compliment, but felt that stray cats and all they symbolized were more significant than politics. In a BBC radio series called "A Hitchhiker's Guide to the Galaxy," someone announces that the whole development of mankind has been an experiment for the benefit of white mice. Certain revelations I have had convince me that true reality — the reality that will blow our minds when we get to that Great Radio Station in the Sky — is of this order. If only subliminally, I have tried to convey this to such of the radio audience as have ears to hear and hearts to understand.

THE SNAILS THAT LAID
THE GOLDEN EGGS

HOST: Everybody knows how the French love to eat snails—escargots, that is—but now a Frenchman has discovered that the *eggs* of snails are even more delicious than their parents, and he's put them on the market. It's a rare event when a new edible animal product is discovered, but snails' eggs are not a solution to world hunger: they cost about forty dollars for a single serving, only a few centimes cheaper than the most expensive caviar. Alice Furlaud has been up in the foothills of the Pyrenees visiting Alain Chatillon, the first person ever to cultivate snails' eggs.

(A crunchy, chewy, rasping sound is heard under the following narration:)

ALICE: That's supposed to be the sound of *Helix aspersa*, or the small grey snail, eating a carrot slice. In actual fact, it's an impersonation by Alain Chatillon himself scraping a knife on an old notebook. His 300,000 snails are all hibernating—on their backs—at Alain's snail farms in different parts of France.

It's not hard to entice Alain out of his shell. He's Napoleonic in size and audacity, and he's delighted that his arrival on the French gastronomic scene is the gourmet event of the year. Snails' eggs are Alain's first adventure in the food business. He describes himself as a self-made man, and for most of his forty-five years he's been a palm reader and a real-estate operator. For dinner in his ultra-modernized house in the tiny mountaintop village of Rennes-le-Château, Alain and I started with a bottle of wine and snails' eggs on toast. *(Alain talks very fast and excitedly.)*

Now he's opening this beautiful little pot of—it's like very large caviar eggs, only a beautiful beige, pinkish beige. About the size of Beluga, very good caviar.

ALAIN: Now your toast is ready.

ALICE: And I'm going to eat the first snails' eggs of my life. I'm making a wish. (*Crunching toast: crunch, crunch.*) Mmmmmmmm!

ALAIN: Fabulous product.

ALICE: It really is yummy. It has a caviar feeling but it's sort of smokier.

(*Sound of crunching under the following narration:*)

ALICE: People have been eating snails in Europe at least since Aristotle's time. In France, for centuries, snails have been grilled alive, flambéed, stuffed, folded into omelets, candied, boiled down to syrup, and prescribed for burns, nose bleeds and constipation. But all this time nobody has thought of eating their eggs, except Alain Chatillon. And since snails lay their eggs only once a year, producing about a hundred eggs weighing a total of three grams, it will cost you 295 francs, or $40, to buy a tiny fifty-gram jar. Alain doesn't think this is much to pay for a food that has magic powers.

ALAIN: Et en plus, vous savez, c'est aphrodisiaque.

ALICE: You have to say that in English.

ALAIN: Because it's a very, very aphrodisiac product.

ALICE: How did you discover that?

ALAIN: It's very simple. Snails' eggs are a symbol of longevity, procreation, and a phallus symbol.

ALICE: A snail is a phallic symbol?

ALAIN: Yeah, yeah, yeah.

ALICE: (*Narrating*) Alain Chatillon saw his first snails' eggs five years ago in a lamasery in Tibet, where he went on a guided tour. They were on a gold plate in the lap of a statue of Buddha—sacred food offered to Buddha and forbidden to mortal tourists. When the guide wasn't looking, Alain stole two of the eggs.

ALAIN: I profit one minute when his back is turned, and I take two eggs in secret.

ALICE: You stole the first eggs you ever had from a lamasery in Tibet?

ALAIN: Um hmm. I eat the two eggs; at the moment I don't appreciate the eggs because they're not prepared. But I think immediately, this is fantastic!

ALICE: *(Narrating)* Alain spent the next four years collecting snails, inventing methods for preserving their eggs and making them taste good, and getting the snails to lay their eggs under controlled conditions. One thing is easy: you don't need to tell male from female snails. Each snail is mother, father and mobile home all in one.

ALAIN: The snails are hermaphrodite. When two snails couple, twenty days after this these two snails put down eggs—this is the hermaphrodite condition.

ALICE: You mean two snails make love, but then each of them goes off and lays eggs, not just one.

ALAIN: Each one put down eggs, twenty days after.

ALICE: *(Narrating)* Clearly snails breed better in captivity than giant pandas—Alain expects to have a million snails this time next year. I asked him what it was like *being* a snail on a snail farm.

ALAIN: These animals are very *difficile*—very finicky, in captivity. They have to have special salad, turnips, carrots, and we give them green grass, and shower baths twice a day to imitate a gentle rain.

ALICE: The eggs they produce in these luxurious conditions, Alain says, are the only comestible product in existence which comes from the union of land-based hermaphrodites. But it takes more than this to convince the chef of a great French restaurant to serve an unknown animal product to his clients. Alain remembers how the chef of the three-star restaurant L'Oasis, at La Napoule, kept him waiting outside the kitchen door for a week before he agreed to taste the snails' eggs.

ALAIN: He say, "What? Snail eggs? You are crazy!" Then he eat on toast with butter and he think, "Effectively, this product is sensationelle! OK," he say, "I put this product immediately in my menu!"

9

ALICE: In the locked laboratory on the top floor of his house, where Alain prepares and bottles his eggs, he protects his secret recipe as feverishly as the medieval alchemists protected their secret recipes for turning base metals into gold. He did allow me to look at snails' eggs being marinated in brine and herbs.

ALAIN: Nobody visits this laboratory. Nobody.

ALICE: Now you're taking a big ladle and dipping it into this vat, and the whole vat is full of snails' eggs. My gosh, Alain, not to be commercial, how much do you think this big bucket of eggs is worth?

ALAIN: About 20,000 francs.

ALICE: That's $2,666 dollars. Alain has already made $100,000 from his snails' eggs. In two years he expects to have made a million dollars. But like the medieval alchemists, Alain feels his snails' eggs have not only brought him riches, but brought him into contact with the mystery of life.

ALAIN: The snail has existed in the world ten million years. It's a dinosaur. And the story of humanity starts a hundred thousand years ago only. If you eat the snails' eggs you eat something very important in eternal life.

ALICE: So far, you can only get a taste of eternity in France. But it should be coming to New York, London, Tokyo and Dallas—by Easter. For National Public Radio, I'm Alice Furlaud, in Rennes-le-Château, France.

It was Linda White, head of the English section of the Canadian Broadcasting Corporation's Paris branch, who told me of the snail egg man. Both of us are always on the alert for the spiritual element in things, and Linda had a feeling Alain Chatillon was a genuine seeker after truth. He's definitely a seeker: he moved to Rennes-le-Château to dig for a hoard of gold reported to have been buried there by the Romans. And even though, in a telephone survey of Tibetan lamas, I couldn't find one who had ever heard of snails' eggs being offered to Buddha, I am sure there's a lot in what Alain says about the eggs containing a fragment of eternal life. I had a hard time, though, convincing him to let me taste even one egg. "You don't need to eat them! I'll tell you all about them!" he declared. There is a type of interviewee who tells you exactly how to do your story, and now, after a ten-hour train and bus journey to this pinnacle in the Pyrenees, I had found one.

DEEP COVE

When people speak English badly the radio rule at NPR is usually to let them speak their native tongue and use a voice-over to simultaneously translate. I have an aversion to voice-overs on radio: they always confuse me. So in interviews I try to drag everybody kicking and screaming into the English language, even if I have to give a lesson, translate and explain to the listener all at once—or invisibly mend the person's speeches in the edit. Such was the case with Alain Chatillon. But it is always restful to come home to the U.S.A. and do reports on people who speak my native language. One of the speakers in the following feature is my mother. The piece was broadcast on Monitoradio, the radio network of the Christian Science Monitor.

HOST: On the Penobscot Bay there's an isolated group of summer houses which may be the last community on the mainland coast of Maine to have so far resisted telephone, television and electric light. But some of the inhabitants are beginning to long for the easier living that comes with telephone poles and light switches. Others are all for keeping their summers as primitive as possible. Alice Furlaud has been hearing the pros and cons from the residents of Deep Cove.

(Sound: waves, seagulls, heard under the following series of voices, known in radio as "vox pop":)

DON THURSTON: Once electricity comes in, then everything that electricity brings will come in.

ANGELICA FANGEL: But I do like a vacuum cleaner.

DORIS THURSTON: When you come up here, you want to be with the rhythm of the universe.

11

MRS. NELSON: And then, of course, we do have this privy. And we don't mind that a bit!

NICK: *(Young boy's voice)* Well, I don't think we want that much. I think that we just need a telephone, so if, like, somebody gets hurt, that you can phone somebody else.

CAROL BUTLER: I don't want to see poles coming down the road. I think they could put it under the ground, or make it attractive somehow, so it's not visible.

ALICE: *(Narrating)* The weathered grey shingle houses on Deep Cove Point are huddled together—only about a hundred feet apart—between the pine forest and the grey, rocky shore. That's because in the 1890s, when they were built, there was no road at all, and everybody had to be near the harbor and their boats. Deep Cove's first summer settlers were William George Tousey, a professor of theology from Boston, and his professor friends. His granddaughter, Katherine Tousey, can just remember him.

KATHERINE TOUSEY: My grandfather was one of the first yachtsmen on the coast of Maine, in 1870 or earlier, and fought in the Civil War, on barkentines, and that's how they discovered this property.

ALICE: What Katherine liked best about Deep Cove summers in her childhood in the 1920s was the total change from city life.

KATHERINE TOUSEY: Even to get here, one would take the steamer overnight from Boston and go to sleep, become unconscious, and when you waked up you found yourself in a whole other universe. You landed in Rockland at 4:00 A.M., and we watched the stevedores tearing down with the baggage, because nothing was mechanical, and they'd get a running start and go up, and then we changed to the little boat which came up the coast stopping from port to port with the mail and with the passengers. And this one, the *Southport*, stopped in Buck's Harbor, and we were met, in my day, by somebody and taken by boat to my grandfather's cottage.

ALICE: *(Narrating)* Katherine's first cousin's widow, Angelica Fangel, a native of Naples, Italy, reacted very differently to *her* first experience of Maine when she came here as a war bride, forty years ago.

ANGELICA FANGEL: I was really appalled by this place, it looked so primitive! It takes a little bit for a European woman to get used to the Maine woods. They're beautiful, but they are *very* primitive. And I remember when I came here, we had a wooden stove, and the water was rainwater, and when there was no rain we had to get the water from the well, and to me it was just terrible.

ALICE: *(Narrating)* Angelica has added a bottled-gas stove and an artesian well, but she'd like all the modern conveniences. Doris Thurston, next door, doesn't want any. Her winters are spent singing and dancing in Miami, and she loves the change of pace at Deep Cove.

DORIS THURSTON: When I came here it was just to be away from humanity, and all this—electricity!—and, you know, people interrupting your life. And here, it's just peace and quiet, and you come back to yourself, and to your roots, and to nature, and to God and to beauty, and Penobscot Bay and fourteen islands, and the sun rising, and the sun setting, and it's just so—you come here for a respite, you know? That's the way I feel.

ALICE: Her brother, Donald Thurston, a professor of oriental studies, doesn't want any electrical devices except one: the nearest public telephone is three miles up a bumpy dirt road, and he'd like Deep Cove to have one shared telephone.

DON THURSTON: Right now there are six elderly widows on this point. There's no phone down here and it takes a good twenty minutes to get to the nearest phone, and then after you get to the phone if you need a doctor it takes longer than that for the doctor to get down here—so I'm not against a phone.

ALICE: But the oldest widow at Deep Cove, Sylvia Nelson, is eighty-six, and she doesn't want a telephone in her tiny cabin. Even the gas lamps, which most of the other residents have, are too bright for her.

MRS. NELSON: I grew up in camps in California, and grew up with kerosene lamps, and I think they're cozy, nice things: what's the matter with them?

ALICE: Mrs. Nelson's way of life is the most Spartan in Deep Cove.

13

MRS. NELSON: When you get up the first thing you do, usually, is build a fire in this cabin we have, and then you have to go outside to the rain barrel and get two teakettles of water. *(Sound of dipper filling kettles)* And then you bring in those teakettles and put them on the stove, and that's what you use for a bath.

ALICE: Carol Butler is the widow of a fourth-generation Deep Cove resident.

CAROL BUTLER: I love the place as it is, but this is the twentieth century, and I think you have to advance with the years, go along with it; I don't think you have to stay in the Dark Ages forever. What would have happened if we had not developed a little bit?

ALICE: But Deep Cove is not the Third World, a place where to be deprived of electricity can deprive its population of education, transport, hospital care. Here, the primitive life is a luxury. But it's the kind of luxury Thoreau experienced at Walden Pond, the kind that can restore the soul. Should it be replaced by the luxury of telephone calls, hi-fis and television? Christopher Kane is a fifth-generation Deep Cove person, aged fourteen. He doesn't miss television down at Deep Cove—well, almost never.

CHRISTOPHER KANE: It's only when I'm bored. But when I'm, like, sailing and everything, if I had television there I wouldn't have done things like walked along the beach, or sailed, or done all sorts of things.

ALICE: And Professor Thurston thinks that once the electric wiring is laid down, TV is inevitable.

DON THURSTON: We will walk down the road and see all the TV boxes on inside the houses instead of seeing these lovely kerosene lanterns and that lovely glow that we all enjoy so much. We will see instead these images flashing and people riveted to their box!

ALICE: And by that time, Katherine Tousey thinks,

KATHERINE TOUSEY: This secluded , silent , thoughtful community will have vanished and become like Boothbay Harbor, a place to float around in stylish manner.

ALICE: At present about half the families of Deep Cove are in favor of modernization, half against. But as their land isn't held in common, no vote need be taken. All that's needed to get the telephone poles marching through the quiet forest of Deep Cove is enough people, with enough money, to put them here. *(Seagulls mew, waves crash.)* I'm Alice Furlaud, on the Penobscot Bay in Maine.

SCREENS

Have you noticed that screens are taking over? How fewer and fewer events happen in the natural world, and more and more things happen on screens? Screens are swallowing up real life in enormous gulps! In Paris, where I live, all the museum art exhibits have video screens scattered among the paintings, and all the fashion shows have movies going on behind the models as they flounce down the runways. There are video games in the once-peaceful Paris cafés, and there's television in the Paris Metro! It's as if people can't be comfortable for a minute without something flashing on a screen nearby. Surgeons operate these days not looking at your insides, but at a movie of your insides on a screen. And I gathered from the Iran Airbus disaster in the Persian Gulf that navy gunners don't even look up at the sky to see what kind of plane they're shooting down: they have to see it on a screen, and the screen gets it all wrong!

Remember NASA's *Challenger* had exploded in midair? They called it a "major malfunction." That cool understatement was what their screens told them. It gives you an idea of how we let screens screen us off from reality.

Television does this best of all. "Isn't Chris Evert a lovely person?" or "I trust Tom Brokaw," we say, looking away from our friends and relations, obscure in the dark living room, at the real people who count, in the lighted magic square. And it's not only Americans to whom people on TV are more real than they are themselves. In India there's a TV series about Krishna and other assorted Hindu gods. They say people prostrate themselves and light incense in front of their TV sets, and in one district when the epic went off the air because of a power failure, viewers burnt down the power station and blocked the main road to Kashmir.

Plato has an analogy for the unenlightened mind: people living all their lives chained inside a cave, so that all they can see is shadows cast by the fire onto the opposite wall. "Would they not assume," asks Plato, "that the shadows they saw were real things?" He should see how we've made his comparison a literal fact of our lives.

And everybody's adding to the shadows in their caves with VHF recorders and videos from video stores and home video cameras, creating more things to watch on screens. And leading the screen invasion of Planet Earth, proliferating as they come, are computers. Computers wouldn't exist without those generations of people who grew up indoors on sunny Saturday mornings watching Kukla, Fran and Ollie. They take in information from a screen like mother's milk. They like seeing their plane reservations come up on that luridly lit screen, and typing their personal letters onto a screen (causing the top of the printed-out letter to read "NWK 1000 SLUG F/B), and buying software toys for their Apples and MacIntoshes so they can see new "menus" on the screen.

There is no computer in my apartment. Not a single screen. No word processor. No television set. And none of those watches or calculators where the numbers appear on little screens. I've hated screens ever since the age of seven, when the movie version of one of my favorite books, *Heidi*, turned out to be full of gangsters chasing Shirley Temple and her grandfather. During most of this terrifying film, my head was in my grandmother's lap. And nearly half a century later, when National Public Radio rashly sent me to the Cannes Film Festival, I sat day after day in movie theaters, eyes shut and fingers in my ears, while decapitations, sadistic sex and other brutalities rolled past on the silver screen. Nowadays, as screens tighten their stranglehold on daily life, my screen phobia is getting worse.

Maybe there are other people out there like me. Maybe we should get together. One day, when all of life is experienced on screens, when screen-watching humanity has become like frogs, who can see only circles, blobs and shadows, we may be useful. If only as plane spotters.

But it's hard to remain pure and not be drawn into the screen-watching circle. For instance, I sneak an occasional look when I'm visiting my mother, who watches the news every night on her dim grey-and-black TV screen. My mother's old cat, Mysty, also a greyish black, is a much stricter anti-screen activist than I am. He is always

17

at her side for the TV ritual, but he never even glances at the television, not even during the cat-food ads. While my mother looks at the screen, he gazes with sheer love up at her face. Which of them is getting the true picture? Plato would know.

A FRENCHMAN'S BEST FRIEND IS AN
ENGLISH BULLDOG

HOST: *(Sue MacGregor of "Woman's Hour" on BBC's Radio 4)* This year is the twentieth anniversary of the founding of a very exclusive French club – the English Bulldog Club of France, or the Club Français du Bulldog Anglais. It's devoted to promoting the ancient breed of dog which a chronicler in Roman times called "the broad-mouthed dog of Britain." The French club has about 200 members who own among them about 300 bulldogs – many fewer than in England or America. The members are, of course, Anglophiles: the courage and doggedness of this jimber-jawed animal are qualities the French often admire in English *people*, in spite of the traditional animosity between the two countries. Alice Furlaud has been investigating the English-bulldog scene in France.

(Sound: a loud wuffle-snuffle, snorting sound with a faint menace in it is heard, then fades under narration.)

ALICE: That is not a maddened pig, or a fire-breathing dragon, or a threshing machine: it's a squat, bowlegged creature somewhat resembling a dog – a very, very ugly dog. In fact, it's Beau, the champion English bulldog of France. He's recovering from a five-flight climb up a Paris staircase. His squashed-in face makes his breathing rather laborious. Can I pet him? I'm going to pet this lovely champion of France – wait! Beau! Beau! He's knocking me down! He's the heaviest – he's quite a small dog but he's heavy. And he's full of wrinkles: his eyes are practically obscured by his nose and his great lower jaw; and he's got a huge collar with great big spikes on it, and he's a kind of a wonderful brindly brown and black, and then white shirt-front and great, solid paws. *(Sound: more snuffle-wuffle, heard under following narration:)*

19

ALICE: Beau was in Paris with his owner, Hélène Denis, a breeder of English bulldogs from Metz, in eastern France.

HÉLÈNE: We have took all the ferocity out, and they are very kind, very nice, well-tempered dogs.

ALICE: You're having puppies at your house soon, aren't you?

HÉLÈNE: Yes, this week, in a few days.

ALICE: Will they be Beau's children?

HÉLÈNE: Yes, of course. Beau has already sired 116 puppies, in two years. He's a popular stud.

ALICE: *(Narrating)* Beau weighs about sixty-five pounds. He was born in Columbia, South Carolina. He's the heavy type of English bulldog they breed in North America. Georges Lacaud, president of the English Bulldog Club of France, likes the compact English model, well under sixty pounds.

GEORGES: I like very much Beau. But I prefer to have here in my house a dog not so fat and always walking and running with me.

ALICE: *(Narrating)* George and his dog, Tewksie, do a lot of running on the beach near their home in Rochefort, on France's Atlantic coast.

GEORGES: *(Over the eager sounds of Tewksie snorting and barking and panting)* C'est bien, Tewksie. Bien! I think I am in a match of rugby because I have Tewksie pushing at me! C'est bien! Good dog! *(More romping and panting.)*

ALICE: Elle comprend "good dog"?

GEORGES: Oh, yes! Good dog, Tewksie! *(Wuffle-wuffle.)*

ALICE: *(Narrating)* Tewksie is a nickname – he was born in Tewksbury, England. His official name is Horace of Kenstaffe. Tewksie played a cameo role in one of the Pink Panther movies: Peter Sellers tripped over him. He is also on the cover of Georges Lacaud's book, *Bulldog* (pronounced here *Bouldug,*), which is full of bulldog history and pictures, including grisly prints of the old sport of bull-baiting, for which the English bulldog was specifically bred.

GEORGES: It is a fabricated race. In the Middle Ages, and even later, they had to have a very low dog. The bull was with the chin on the ground, and there was a space between the chin and the horns, and it was necessary for the bulldog to creep along the ground under the horns and then to smash! on the muzzle of the bull.

ALICE: *(Narrating)* These days, English bulldogs are only bred for dog shows, but they're still a man-made race. Left to themselves, they wouldn't breed at all.

GEORGES: If the female is very high in the hind legs, and if the male is very low, you must help them.

ALICE: What do you do?

GEORGES: If a man wants to kiss a very tall woman he gets a chair. He gets up on a chair, don't he? Well, the bulldog can't stay on the chair, so you help him not to lose his balance. Of course. It's the same thing. Not to kiss, but to . . .

ALICE: *(Interrupting swiftly with the narration)* But Georges wants to give English bulldogs a more natural image. When the English Bulldog Club of France was founded twenty years ago by the Princess of Bourbon Parme, having an English bulldog was a joke, like keeping an alligator in your bathtub.

GEORGES: When we took the club in hand, we intended to show that the English bulldog was the monster with the kind heart. Not a toy, but a dog which was able to think, and to be with you, and more than other dogs, certainly.

(Sound of Tewksie eating his dinner—an eager, Rabelaisian slurping, grunting, wolfing sound—is heard under following narration:)

ALICE: Tewksie shared the extravagant French dinner provided by Georges Lacaud—local scallops, coquilles St. Jacques, in a rich sauce. This happy breed of dog eats well in France, a country where dogs are welcome in restaurants. During dinner Hélène Denis telephoned from Paris.

GEORGES: Felicitations! Oui! bonne nouvelle pour la race, pour le Club . . . *(His delighted voice fades down, babbling on in French under my narration.)*

ALICE: He's congratulating her on the birth, by cesarian section, of eight puppies sired by Beau. A good reason for champagne.

GEORGES: Ready? Pop! *(The pop of an especially exuberant cork.)*

(Sound of snoring—an extravagantly resigned snore—of an exhausted dog, is heard under the final bit of narration.)

ALICE: Thus, as it must to all dogs, sleep came to Horace of Kenstaffe—call him Tewksie. He's lying on a bare wooden shelf in his kennel, on his back, front paws in the air. Did you ever see a bulldog dreaming? Well, I did. *(Whispers:)* I'm Alice Furlaud, in Rochefort, France.

(Fade up snoring over gentle lullaby music.)

SHAKESPEARE AND COMPANY

HOST: *(On the Deutsche Welle program "Across the Atlantic")* The most ancient-looking building on the river side of the Latin Quarter in Paris is an American bookshop. For thirty-three years, owner George Whitman has run Shakespeare and Company, just across from Notre Dame, as a combination public library and youth hostel. Alice Furlaud is a regular browser.

ALICE: *(On location)* Shakespeare and Company has beamed walls and a wavy roof line, and it looks as if Hansel and Gretel might pop in any minute to buy a book on witchcraft. Outside in the rain, leaning against one of the cartons of cheap books, is a waterlogged bulletin board with messages from lost souls. One says, "Brad! I'm leaving for England tomorrow. Please come and meet me there soon! Kathy." You can get an elderly Penguin book from the outdoor book-shelf for about a dollar, or three for $2.50, and there's even a box of free books. Here's volume 1 of *The Human Soul*, by Isaiah Twomey, and a manual on *How to Operate the Mixmaster*. Inside, owner George Whitman, a sixtyish, leprechaunlike Bostonian with a goatee, is sell-ing books and receiving homage.

ALICE: George, I have a book which I bought here the first year I came to Paris, and I'm going to give it back to you because I think it's got to belong to this bookstore. It's called *Murder in Paris*, by Alice Campbell.

GEORGE: That's the first book you ever bought here! Well now, I just wonder if that's one of the books that I acquired from the library of Gertrude Stein. She had a most amazing collection of detective stories.

ALICE: *(Narrating)* Gertrude Stein and Hemingway and James Joyce, and other English-speaking writers used to hang around another Shakespeare and Company bookshop, further inland on the Rue de l'Odéon, in the 1920s and '30s. Its owner, Sylvia Beach, published James Joyce's *Ulysses*. Some Parisians accuse George Whitman of pretending that Sylvia Beach chose him as her successor. He denies this.

GEORGE: No, it was when I had my bookstore in Boston and heard about Shakespeare and Company, I always thought that was the one name for a literary bookstore. I half thought of mentioning to her the idea of taking over Shakespeare and Company, and I never did. One reason was, I thought if she said no, I could never do it.

ALICE: *(Narrating)* But the new Shakespeare and Company has inherited one or two traditions from the old one. For instance, the picturesque jumble the books are in; there's no discernible alphabetical, or other, order.

GEORGE: The whole basic principle is bookstore serendipity: You never find what you want, but in looking for what you want you find something that you didn't know you want, at least as good if not better.

(Sound of footsteps going slowly up a wooden staircase.)

ALICE: *(Narrating)* Another Sylvia Beach tradition that's carried on by George Whitman is hospitality for young writers. I found my way up a very rickety staircase between tottering walls of books to the well-named Old Smoky Reading Room, to meet George's ten or twelve guests who were camping out there.

YOUNG MAN: I was a reader here for two years. I used to come over and read in the library. And financial circumstances forced me to ask George to let me stay here for a while, and now I have my dog here with me. She's just come from the States.

ALICE: Well, this is the most tiny little kitchen, sort of wedged in between bookshelves. And you're making a sandwich . . .

YOUNG MAN: Bread and butter, it's the staple here. It's all we eat: bread, butter and cheese.

ALICE: There are books on top of the stove, there are books on top of the refrigerator . . .

YOUNG WOMAN: There are even books on top of the toilet.

ALICE: And where do you all sleep?

YOUNG MAN: Between the shelves. We just kind of slide out a book and hop in.

ALICE: *(Narrating)* At the regular Monday night poetry readings, it sometimes appears doubtful if this new lost generation of American writers at Shakespeare and Company can measure up to the Sylvia Beach, Hemingway and Fitzgerald crowd.

(Applause at the reading.)

A POET NAMED MARCO POLO: I think that I will close with another poem that's got to do with Shakespeare and Company. "Tradition. Shakespeare and Company, Paris, France. Grey, rainy day. But each Sunday afternoon at four, warmth of congenial conversation pours freely from the merrily steaming pot. . . ."

(Sound: chatter, mostly in English, at the tea party.)

ALICE: *(Narrating)* The Shakespeare and Company Sunday tea parties do have an intellectual tone. Among the cracked cups and the French animal crackers people really do come and go, talking of, among other things, Michelangelo. At any rate, George Whitman— as distantly related to Walt Whitman as his bookshop is related to the original Shakespeare and Company—has a sense of mission. He clearly feels that his bookshop is an institution, an important part of the literary life of Paris.

GEORGE: We started on a shoestring: I bought my store for five hundred dollars. This is now worth a million dollars. It's no gratification to me, the fact that it's worth a million dollars—that means nothing to me. I'm going to give it away and make a foundation.

ALICE: *(Narrating)* George Whitman does not disclose how much money Shakespeare and Company is making. But he does admit to being a bit swamped.

GEORGE: I've had terrible problems. We have too many customers here! I love to read books! And here I am writing out orders, doing invoices, accounts, when I've got a beautiful wife and a very charming baby and a nice kitten and a dog, and I like walking and reading— and here I am just being a businessman. A *petit bourgeois* businessman!

ALICE: *(Narrating)* In the midst of the book rat race, George Whitman sees himself as a contemplative type.

GEORGE: I can't trace the history of this bookstore before the year 1600. At that year it was a monastery. It was called La Maison de Moutiers. And I'll let you know a little secret of mine: that I am the only surviving monk in this monastery.

(Notre Dame bells again, drowned out by aggressive traffic, over:)

ALICE: From the heart of the American literary scene in Paris, I'm Alice Furlaud.

THE MARTIAL ART OF THE MARKET

Broadcast on CBC's "Food Show," autumn 1985.

ALICE: My first experience of the contest of wills which is shopping in a Paris outdoor market, was when I asked for potatoes in the Marché de Buci. The vegetable man weighed them out. But when he saw that I hadn't brought a shopping bag with me, he barked out "Ah!" as only a furious Frenchman can say "Ah!" and dumped the potatoes off the scale onto the ground. Later I learned that the stall holders in the Marché de Buci are famous for their bad tempers. One Christmas Eve I saw a fight there which went as far as the customer grabbing the vendor by the front of his smock and lifting him several inches off the ground before they were separated. The Marché de Buci is in a little square which is the site of the Café Momus in *La Bohème* – if you remember the second act where a lot of hot-tempered dialogue is sung and spoken by the artists and their girlfriends. So maybe the irritable character of this market is just another Paris tradition.

Each of the eighty-four markets of Paris, in fact, has its traditions and character. The market in the Place Maubert, across from Notre Dame on the Left Bank, hasn't changed much, give or take a few hundred automobiles, since the days just before the French Revolution, when housewives had a demonstration there to protest the price of bread. The vendors in the Marché St. Honoré are known for their glacial haughtiness. The Marché d'Aligre, on the east side of Paris, is known for its cheapness. And the street market where I live, near the Paris city hall, the Hôtel de Ville, has some of the qualities of all of the above.

27

I've just come back from the daily battle there. As usual, I ran the frightening gauntlet between the stalls with the vendors like two rows of vultures uttering their hoarse, aggressive cries. There was the old fruit seller who always taunts me, "Don't buy these grapes! You can't afford them!" At the first vegetable stand I was paralyzed trying to keep my eye on everything at once: the autumn vegetables arranged in gaudy patterns, the prices overhead on a clothesline, the scale which the stall man was leaning on slightly with his elbow, my change, the fellow shoppers shoving me aside, the delicatessen next door where the usual ruffians were pulling the legs off the hot chickens rotating on an outdoor spit. ("Why don't they steal the whole chicken?" the shop owner often complains. "It would be less depressing than mutilating them!") And now that I've climbed up to my apartment, put down my shopping basket and had a good cry, I've made a resolution: I'm going to imitate my French neighbors, who love the cut and thrust of the market. Tomorrow I'm going to go into that market fighting. I'm going to say "Ah!" if they give me a single brussels sprout I don't like; I'm going to count my change slowly and suspiciously; and I'm going to keep my place in line if I have to knock somebody down with an eggplant. For the Food Show, this is Alice Furlaud, going native in Paris!

TRUFFLES IN TROUBLE

One of my favorite features of Paris is that it is a city of seasons. There's a season for everything from drag races to mushrooms— autumn for the latter, of course—but there is one special mushroom, the morille, *whose season is May. On the first of May people give each other lilies-of-the-valley, and on the first of August so many people go off on vacation that the streets are deserted. On New Year's Eve everybody—nearly everybody, that is, and not just the rich—eats pâté de foie gras, liberally laced with tiny fragments of truffles.*

The truffle is a strong-smelling, black fungus about the size of a golf ball, found only in small corners of Europe near the roots of oak trees. It cannot be cultivated or imitated, although the Japanese keep trying; and it can only be found by dogs or pigs. The truffle season of 1985, when I went down to Cahors to investigate this extremely expensive mushroom, was the worst the truffle merchants had known for years. Only ten tons, as opposed to the usual fifty or sixty, had been unearthed in all of France that winter. I especially remember, on that trip to southwest France, the old peasants, pinched from the cold in the windy village marketplace, silently offering their baskets of one or two truffles; and the contrasting scene in the warm, glittery restaurant in Cahors where truffles were served to well-fed towns- people. But the creatures that haunt me the most are the miserably exploited truffle pigs. I started the "All Things Considered" piece with the host saying something about Alice being out in the woods "sniff- ing out the possibilities," and followed this with the desperately eager snorting, sniffing, rooting sound of one of these poor pigs. Over this was heard:

ALICE: *(Narrating)* That's a little white pig with pink ears snuffling with his snout deep in the pebbly soil, in an oak forest near Cahors.

29

She's following the strange, powerful scent of truffles. Her elderly peasant owners, Monsieur and Madame Foureste, are close behind her. The pig's pulling so enthusiastically on her leash that Madame Foureste is having a hard time holding her.

MADAME FOURESTE: *(With pig excitedly sniffing and snuffling in background)* Cherche la! Cherche la!

ALICE: Madame Foureste gives her a clout on the head *(This can be clearly heard, after which the pig squeaks in protest)* and says, "Keep looking! Keep looking! Look here! Look here!" she's saying. *(Another clout, pig snuffles and squeaks.)*

ALICE *(Narrating)*: A full-grown pig would be impossible for an old woman to control on a leash, so this pig will be killed and eaten in the spring, and next fall the Fourestes will buy another to take her place. Pigs need no training to track down truffles: the smell of this unique mushroom called *la truffe* drives them mad with excitement. Some people down here say a female pig is an especially avid truffle hunter, because the truffle contains the hormones and smell of a male wild boar. Other experts say this is hogwash. But it's clear that this pig, given half a chance, would completely pig out on truffles.

ALICE: *(At the scene)* And pig is digging, she's pushing, she's making a real trench, a deep trench with her snout—*(the pig squeaks sharply)*. The pig's protesting as she was kicked aside just as she was about to swallow the one truffle she found all afternoon. The snout was nearly quicker than the eye, but Madame Foureste snatched the truffle away just in time. It was only about the size of a marble, but with truffles selling at $120 a pound, even the pig who made it all possible is not going to get one.

MADAME FOURESTE: Elle est là, la truffe! *(Pig: grunt-grunt.)* Prends-là, prends le maïs: il est là!

ALICE: *(Narrating)* But even with their gourmet pig surviving on garbage, the Fourestes can't earn a living from truffles alone. The vineyard on their twenty-seven acres of rough and rocky land has to be their main source of income. The people in this region who do earn a living from truffles are the many truffle merchants in and around Cahors, the medieval town on the river Lot, which is the business and canning center for French truffles.

(Sound: the market. Wary murmurs, sudden bursts of gabbling in which can be detected the pleasantly harsh accent of the southwest, heard under following narration:)

ALICE: They buy most of the fresh truffles they preserve and export at the weekly winter truffle market in the village of Lalbenque, twelve miles down the river from Cahors and about the same distance from the Fourestes' oak forest. This wild part of France is untouched by tourist hands, and it's hard to believe that this bleak little hilltop village is the truffle center of the world, supplying all the grand restaurants and food snobs from Dallas to Tokyo. About thirty old women and men are standing behind rough plank tables, each with a little basket of what look like clods of frozen earth – truffles from their own backyards. Milling around the little marketplace are sixty or so buyers from all over southwest France – all men, and almost all wearing black berets. They approach the baskets cautiously, look at the truffles, smell them, and then stand aside and gossip about them.

TRUFFLE MERCHANTS: Il est une truffe qui vient de l'extérieur, oui, oui, oui, etc. *(Sound of their voices fades under.)*

ALICE: These old truffle hands are outraged by some inferior truffles they say have been sneaked in from Spain or Italy. But how can they tell these from the others, when by strict tradition the truffles are sold with all the earth still on them, and you're not allowed to touch one? No one would tell me. Not even the "King of Truffles," as he's called here, Jacques Pébeyre. Monsieur Pébeyre's family has been trafficking in truffles in Cahors for four generations. His great-grandfather supplied truffles to the czar of Russia. *(To Monsieur Pébeyre:)* How can you tell whether it's a truffle or a lump of coal under all that earth?

MONSIEUR PÉBEYRE: No problem. No, no problem. *(Laughs.)* A truffle is a truffle, with earth or without earth. For a buyer of truffles, a truffle is a truffle.

ALICE: When a truffle is not really a truffle, though, is when it's preserved. When it's those tasteless little black chips you get in a can of foie gras, for instance. The newly dug-up truffle can only be experienced in the winter, and it only keeps for a week. So when you're invited to participate in the fresh truffle mystery, you are awed.

Monsieur Pébeyre, you're choosing a truffle to give to me; it's like being given a diamond! I don't know whether I should accept it.

MONSIEUR PÉYBEYRE: This is to make a little salade, with oil of truffles and lemon: Just a little salade.

ALICE: This is a beautiful thing. I think I'm going to go right out and sell this for five hundred dollars. I'm not going to make a salad out of it! *(Both of us laugh, he more heartily than I, who was really tempted to grab the thing and run.)*

ALICE: *(Narrating)* In fact, I wrapped my truffle in a piece of the local newspaper, the *Dépêche du Lot*, and took it to the truffle restaurant of Cahors, where the chef used the whole black nobbly truffle to make me a salad that would have cost the average Frenchman a week's rent.

(The next voice you hear is me, alternately munching and muttering into a microphone which I am trying to hide under my napkin. I always find this terribly embarrassing, especially when alone in a crowded and grand restaurant, saying "yum-yum," etc., to myself.)

ALICE: Hmmmm. It's very strange, crunchy and *very* perfumed. You can smell it while you're eating it, and it's salty, and it has the real taste of the actual roots, the bowels of the earth, extraordinary, right out of *Orpheus and Eurydice*.

CHEF: The truffle is a gift of God.

ALICE: So said the chef, Patrick Lannes, in the restaurant kitchen.

CHEF: Sometimes in the morning I catch a truffle, and I smell. It's a kind of drug! If you have an entire marriage with a truffle, the flavor you have in your nose, it's something fantastic!

ALICE: Is this why they call it an aphrodisiac? It seems to have magic powers!

CHEF: Yes, it's also what many people call magic powers, yes. *(Laughs shyly.)*

(Oh dear. I always seem to be asking people in the French food world if things are aphrodisiac and using the rather coy euphemism of "magic powers." My excuse is that in a radio interview with people who speak English poorly, there's always the fear that the conversation will be boring. When this happens in food reporting, I guess I bring in the old aphrodisiac theme as a sort of desperate

measure. Or maybe I just happen to choose foods that are aphrodisiacs. If this offends you, skip the oyster script a little further on.)

ALICE: Monsieur Lannes has used his magic powers as a chef to create a whole menu of truffle dishes: truffle omelettes, truffles in champagne sauce, truffles in puff paste. But I didn't have the heart to order the truffled roast pork: it could have been somebody I knew. *(Sound: pig snuffling under sign-out.)* For National Public Radio, I'm Alice Furlaud, in Cahors, France. *(More snuffling and snorting and grunting on the part of the pig.)*

ONLY FAIR HARVARD

I stole that last line from my father, posthumously. It was one of millions of such throwaway remarks he used to mutter. This one he muttered to a waiter who recommended the turtle soup the day after Daddy had started to put his drink down on a footstool in a strange house and the footstool walked away; it was a giant pet turtle.

It was to somehow represent my father at his quietly beloved Harvard that I proposed to National Public Radio to do a feature on the college's 350th birthday in 1986. It was a slightly depressing experience. I kept passing a certain corner of Garden Street which reminded me of a day nearly forty years before, when my father was visiting me at Radcliffe. At that corner, he suddenly dropped my arm and rushed up to a tiny, bent old man who was about to step off the curb. "Professor Copeland?" said Daddy, with an eagerness I had never heard in his voice before, "Frederic Nelson, 1916. May I walk home with you?" I followed them, forgotten. My father was in his sixties, rather frail himself, and very, very shy. But seeing the famously irascible old professor of English transformed him back into the Harvard student who had been thrilled by the privilege of being a regular guest at Professor Copeland's "evenings."

Not that such an encounter couldn't happen at the Harvard of the 1980s. But to me in 1986, Harvard no longer felt just the place to discover eternal values. The Harvard of my father's day and mine knew it was the greatest, but knew it without the showoff self-consciousness I felt there on the college's 350th anniversary. Harvard was bristling with such importance, so many new libraries and "centers" of so many modern designs; so many computer scientists and other well-heeled wizards; and as for the Business School, it had gotten definitely above itself. All around Harvard Square were new and glittery shopping plazas, hotels and motels; and further from the center, the old wooden houses with their dog-eared roofs were all painted trendy "decorator" colors, probably called raspberry and avocado. They looked more suitable for business consultants than the old ladies and professorial types who used to appear on their front porches.

There were good changes, of course. When Daddy arrived as a freshman in 1912, financed by his clergyman father, an old female Cambridge cousin and summer jobs on newspapers, there was a visible difference between rich and poor Harvard students. The gap between the likes of Daddy and his friends in their cheap Cambridge boarding houses and the classmates who were driven back from vacations by chauffeurs in huge cars, smothered in lap robes, was vast. It's a good thing that blue jeans cover a multitude of millionaires, as well as scholarship students. And now half the students are women. Although it makes me a little sad that my own college, Radcliffe, has been more or less submerged in this process, things are a lot better than when Daddy and his friends marched in the Boston suffragette protest parade and were jeered at by the rich Bostonians standing on the steps of the Union Club.

The "All Things Considered" host who read (and rewrote somewhat) the introduction to this piece was Margot Adler, a good friend and one of the greater NPR geniuses and free spirits.

HOST: Unless you've been on some remote island, you've probably noticed that Harvard University has been holding a four-day-long celebration for its 350th birthday this week. The city of Cambridge, Massachusetts, has been flooded with all sorts of alumni and some nonalumni, like England's Prince Charles. The activities will continue throughout tomorrow. Alice Furlaud prepared this report:

(Sound of cheering, and the shouted announcement: "Ladies and gentlemen! The Harvard! University! Band!!" And the band blares away, playing "With Crimson in Triumph Flashing," a rousing football song. Over this you heard:)

ALICE: *(Narrating)* Harvard's birthday party has brought so many important people to town that fourteen security agencies have been called in, plus Scotland Yard, of course. There's a huge assortment of pleasures to choose from: fireworks, boat concerts, dances, poetry readings, and, fittingly, lectures by one hundred Harvard professors. Subjects range from "The Language of the French Revolution" to one called "Space-Age Materials in Crowns and Bridges," over at the Dental School. The celebrations began outdoors, down by the River Charles, in the rain. The helium-inflated triumphal arch, which was supposed to stretch across the river to Boston, ended in shreds; and the laser displays weren't colorfast. But Harvard had hired all sorts of cheery musicians, including a women's samba band and the *Yale* Russian Choir. The Harvard Band was taken over by a group of alumni of all ages. Chris Kelly was playing the trumpet.

CHRIS KELLY: *(Just audible over the thump-thump of a huge drum)* I think there are some of us who are probably pushing sixty, but not much older than that.

ALICE: Have you had much time to practice together?

CHRIS KELLY: Oh, none at all! We had a rehearsal this afternoon. And that was it.

ALICE: How did you do?

CHRIS KELLY: Ha, ha, ha, ha! Well, about like you'd expect for a bunch of lawyers and doctors and other washed-up musicians who don't play nearly enough.

(Sound: thumping of drums, excited babble from the crowd, ending with my friend Anne Wyman, former editor of the Boston Globe, *belting out the last line of a song.)*

ANNE: Three cheers for Harvard, and down! with! Yale!

ALICE: *(Narrating)* The evening didn't have the dignity you might expect at a Harvard occasion, but it did have diversity, a quality Harvard is famous for. Harvard's buildings are a jumble of architecture, from the stately red-and-white University Hall by Bulfinch, to the stark white Carpenter Center by Le Corbusier, and the tiny, triangular Lampoon Building with a funny face made out of its windows. Harvard hasn't got a campus, like other colleges: it's got a "yard." Classes are held in the very place where in 1636 they fenced out the cows, and where the first freshman class of nine students were regularly beaten and complained of goat droppings in their hasty pudding. Yesterday Harvard Yard was cordoned off for a solemn convocation featuring the Prince of Wales. The faculty were all dressed up in a varied collection of gowns and hoods and flat mortarboard hats. Prince Charles wore this costume, too, only his was dazzling with gold embroidery. His speech delighted everybody by flattering Harvard outrageously.

PRINCE CHARLES: The suspense of this mammoth occasion has been killing me! *(Sound of huge outdoor audience roaring with polite laughter.)* You have devised an exquisite torture for the uninitiated *(more delighted laughter)*; but I realize now that all my character-building education, which I have endured in the past, has prepared me for this one great occasion. *(More laughs and clapping over following narration:)*

ALICE: The prince's presence here was not, as you might think, because Harvard is on the Charles River, but because he graduated from England's Cambridge University, just like John Harvard, the young clergyman who left Harvard its first endowment of 400 books. Now Harvard has about four *million* books, most of which are in the huge Widener Library, which faced the prince as he spoke, with its great expanse of steps covered with chrysanthemums in the Harvard colors, red and white.

PRINCE CHARLES: I am particularly pleased and proud to be standing here in the Yard. I have heard a great deal about Harvard—who hasn't? I have also heard of Yale. *(Sound: after a fractionally shocked silence, more laughs—the satisfied laughter of a large and privileged and possibly snob-infested audience, which is about to eat a large and privileged lunch. This laughter and clapping fades under narration.)*

ALICE: If all this sounds like too much fuss over a mere college birthday, you have to realize that Harvard is the oldest college on this continent, unless you count Saint Thomas Aquinas University in Santo Domingo, which was founded in 1538. Six U.S. presidents went to Harvard, and so did all sorts of other impressive people, like Henry David Thoreau, Ralph Waldo Emerson, John Dos Passos, Robert Frost, and John Reed—the only American who's buried in the Kremlin wall. One of Harvard's twenty-nine Nobel Prize winners, James Watson, discovered the structure of the genetic code, possibly the most important scientific breakthrough of this century. And no other university in America has a law school, *and* a medical school, *and* a business school, *and* a famous art museum *and* three and a half billion dollars.

The philosopher William James, class of 1869, said, "The true Harvard is the invisible Harvard in the souls of her more truth-seeking, and independent, and often very solitary sons." It probably didn't occur to him that there would ever be Harvard daughters. But Harvard's new coeducational status is the greatest change in the college since James's day.

Whether you're a Harvard woman or a Harvard man, you probably feel that yours has been a strange and unique education, which somehow involves you more in the power and glory of this country than a graduate of any other college. Sarah Bicks does, and she's only a Harvard junior:

SARAH BICKS: You're part of Harvard; you're part of one of the best institutions in the world, and it rubs off on you *(laughs shyly)*. It does! There is an arrogance that some people consider — don't like at all — but that gives Harvard kids an incredible confidence when they graduate.

ALICE: *(Narrating)* Sarah should be on hand for Harvard's 400th birthday. The keynote speaker will no doubt be Prince William, and Harvard will probably be celebrating itself with the same fervor, only more so.

(Sound: a big crowd, accompanied by the Harvard Band, has been singing Harvard's hymn, "Fair Harvard," during this last bit of narration, and now the song swells up.)

CROWD: By these festival rites, from the age that is past, to the age that is going before. . . . *(Song comes up under the sign-out.)*

ALICE: For National Public Radio, I'm Alice Furlaud, in Cambridge, Massachusetts.

DOGGING THE FOOTSTEPS
OF THE FRENCH

Visiting Paris? Disconcerted by being scorned in the shops, scur-
ried past disdainfully in the streets, and generally made to feel about
as welcome as a fully uniformed German circa 1943? Try my approach
to the Parisian-in-the-street: talk to his dog. A new Paris will open
for you – the lovely Paris of the serious nut-case animal freaks. More
passionate dog lovers walk the streets of Paris than those of any city
I know: there are about eight million dogs in France. Of these, about
two-thirds are mongrels, and they are the ones you should greet
with a comment like, "O, quel adorable woof-woof": not the *chiens
de race*, or pedigreed dogs. I find that when I ask the ordinary, sin-
cere French mongrels if they're "having a nice walk" ("Tu fais une
bonne promenade?"), their worried, hurried, sourpuss owners go all
soft and modestly proud and friendly. Never the owners of pure-
bred dogs, who walk coolly past me without breaking step. These
Parisians seem much less attached to their pets than mongrel owners.
I once saw a tiny poodle killed by two cars on the Boulevard Saint-
Germain. My husband was nearly killed himself, trying to stop the
second car, and I went to pieces. But the dog's owners, a little girl
and her mother, reacted as if they had merely dropped their ice-
cream cones in the street. Leaving the corpse behind, they walked
away, the mother remarking: "Too bad, we only had this one a year."
If that had been a mutt, he would have been given a full military
funeral.

The most beloved, and the ugliest, Paris dog I've met on my strolls
is Lewis, a grizzled, Beaglesque creature wearing a happy smile. Lewis
embodies in one dog the battle of good and evil which rages in the
French pet world. He and his owner, a chef called Beatrice Ayral,
met when Lewis was hurled out of a speeding car at her feet, his

throat cut from ear to ear. Ms. Ayral got him to a vet just in time. Now, the huge scar still visible, Lewis leads a pampered life in a Les Halles apartment with Beatrice and her ex-stray cat, Charlie. Lewis spends his vacations in Spain or Italy, where the sight of him riding proudly in a gondola is, Ms. Ayral says, unforgettable.

I drew abreast of an almost equally hideous dog one day – an aged, obese, semi-bloodhound waddling across the Quai de la Tournelle, her huge teats brushing the ground as she rolled along. She was led by an equally shapeless and ragged old woman. When I ventured some mendacious compliment on the dog, the old woman replied with dignity, "Madame, this dog is the dog of Louise de Vilmorin!" *Louise de Vilmorin?* Grande dame, author, cultural guru, great and good friend of Andre Malraux, with whom she was photographed next to his grand piano, an elegant Siamese cat or two out of focus in the background? It was as if a bag lady on the Bowery had said, "This is the dog of Claire Booth Luce."

In adjusting your street consciousness to dog level, it's important that your motives be pure. You are, in noticing his pet, getting closer to the Inner Parisian: but as in Zen and the Art of Anything, it only works if you approach the dog for himself, not in hopes of making friends with the person at the other end of the leash. I am a genuine mongrel-dog enthusiast, but anybody can become one if he focuses his awareness and lets love happen. I do tell an occasional lie to explain why I'm admiring some dreadful-looking dog: "Your dog reminds me of my dog," I say, silently apologizing to the ghosts of all my former dogs.

French dogs respond to greetings with more eye sparkling, wriggling and wagging than the dogs of other nations. But their owners open up like Japanese paper flowers in a glass of water. I have even gladdened the hearts of the grim-looking women I think of as concierges because they wear aprons in the street, by cooing to their dogs. These always seem to be black and white, tubby, and stiff-legged, always wearing hand-knit, emerald green sweaters. I have made friends with a neighborhood beggar – not by buying his songs, which he writes on scraps of graph paper, but by dialogues with his dogs, Socrates and Suzy. Once I delighted an irascible old neighbor by returning his wandering mutt who, curiously, had "Chirac" inscribed on his collar. Other neighbors say that the owner often takes his dog to the imposing front of the Hôtel de Ville where Jacques Chirac presides as mayor of Paris, and loudly commands the dog, "Lie down, Chirac! Heel, Chirac!" —but I have never caught him doing this. Chirac is one of the very few Paris dogs I know who has a French name. I have never met a dog called Pompidou —a name more suitable for a French poodle than a prime minister. But except for a few internationally named dogs, such as Rex, Prince, and Sultan, the names of almost all the French dogs I encounter reflect the Anglo-Saxon snob element lying deep in the French character: Beauty, Bobby, Mickey, Snoopy, Pickwick, Queenie, Alfred, Rambo, Willy, Dolly, Lady . . . (Lady, a mixed terrier who works with her owner in a shop on my street, once attempted suicide by jumping off the Pont Neuf. The river police fished her out in front of the Samaritaine department store.) I've met a taxi driver's dog called Tommy in honor of "le oo," and a little tattle-tale grey dog called Penalty —an English sporting word which last year was reprovingly listed as "unnecessary" by the Académie Française.

The Académie Française, or just the French passion for precision in language, may be responsible for the distinction between a *bâtard*, a dog whose parents were pure-bred dogs of two different known races, and a *corniaud*, the details of whose racial mix is unknown. Some proud owners will tell you their mongrel is a fancy-sounding breed, for instance a *Berger Belge*, or Belgian shepherd, a title which covers a multitude of multibreed animals.

My favorite Belgian shepherd is Whiskey, a barrel-shaped, lop-eared neighbor who spends most of his day lying on the sidewalk in front of his owners' bakery on the Rue des Archives, acting as a sort of neighborhood greeter. Passersby who have to step over him murmur "Allô, Whiskey!" as a matter of routine. The family who owns this boulangerie were cold to me for several years, until I began asking after Whiskey, when a flood of fond information poured from them and we became friends. Whiskey has a heart condition and is on a "diet" which includes two *tartines* a day —a slice of buttered rye bread and one of whole wheat. He cannot resist his master's chocolate Bavarian cream and *tartes aux fraises*: "He never eats the crust; just the strawberries and the crème Chantilly." With this kind of canine cuisine widespread, no wonder the house dog I met in a café near the Madeleine wore a sign on his collar: "Don't feed me sugar lumps: I am a diabetic."

Warning: the entente cordiale you attain through Parisian dogs can become more cordial than you might wish. Back in 1949, at the outset of my "Junior Year Abroad," I made the acquaintance, at the student café Chez Dupont on the Place Saint-Michel, of an enormous, black-faced German shepherd. My friendship with this animal was taken in quite the wrong way by the three young men with him, to whom I didn't pay much attention until I was in their basement apartment and it was too late. I had only been in Paris a week, and had romantic notions of what an evening with French students would be like: reciting Clément Marot, strumming on lutes, etc. But I had been so busy cuddling the dog that I hadn't realized that not only were these types not students at all (one of them was the trumpet player at the Tabou, the most fashionable smoke-and-jazz emporium in town, and a gypsy to boot), but that they had another sort of evening in mind. They locked me in and started ripping off my Peck & Peck tweed suit, and during the scuffle they threatened to order the German shepherd to rape me. I was incredibly relieved when a neighbor, who heard me screaming, persuaded them through the keyhole to let me out. But looking back on the experience, I don't believe that nice dog would have done any such thing.

THE DWARF CEMETERY

(Sound: French demonstrators with high voices cry out "solidarité" and other slogans.)

ALICE: (Narrating) It was a dwarf demonstration. By that, I mean not a small demonstration, but a demonstration by small people. There were about two hundred dwarfs, and they managed to block the Champs Elysées for two and a half minutes! They were protesting a plan, recently announced by the mayor of Paris, to close down the Cimetière de Poche, or Pocket Cemetery. Since the seventeenth century, this cemetery has been reserved exclusively for dwarfs. The city now plans to use the site as part of a new barracks for the Paris riot police. Investigating the cause of this demonstration, I hurried over to the pocket cemetery to be sure to get there before the bulldozers.

ALICE: (Continuing on location at the cemetery in an awed, hushed voice) The dwarf cemetery is known to few tourists and it's well worth a visit. It's in the southern Montsouris section of Paris, and once you've ducked into the trellis gateway here (spooky hinges squeak), you've entered another world. These grounds aren't so much landscaped as manicured, and the walks—little mosaic paths between the graves—are edged with lovely dwarf tulips and bonsai box hedges.

MONSIEUR TRITAULT: (High, squeaky voice) Ah, de toute façon moi je suis trop grand pour être enterré dans ce cimetière, hein . . . C'est vraiment dommage . . .

ALICE: Ah oui.
(As Monsieur Tritault gabbles on, Alice continues to narrate on location.)

43

ALICE: The cemetery caretaker is Monsieur Emmanuel Tritault. He's been showing me around. He says he's nearly four feet high and that's really too tall to be allowed to be buried in this cemetery. But he's hoping that the dwarfs' protests will influence the right-wing Mayor Chirac to spare this cemetery, if only because General de Gaulle's little-known younger brother is buried here. He was apparently about two and a half feet high and he was a pioneer in lighter-than-air flight. *(Awed:)* And here he is . . . *(footsteps)* . . . Nénuphar de Gaulle . . . and the epitaph just says, "Adieu, Petite Grandeur"—Farewell, Little Grandeur . . . Oh, my gosh!

(Monsieur Tritault chatters on in the background.) Monsieur Tritault is saying that there are all classes of society in this cemetery. They have the graves of, uh . . . several chimney sweeps and a duke . . . and, naturally, quite a few circus performers. He's showing me this one—let's see . . . Le Pygmie, 1820–1882. And here's an elaborate-looking family vault sort of like thing, with carving—when they say "just like lace," this really *is* lace. And oh, no—it's the vault reserved for the court fools of the kings of France. And here inside you can just see one—an epitaph. It says, "Bravo, César!" Further along here, let's see, there's *Pépin le Bref*, Pippin the Brief—and he was apparently a second cousin of Tom Thumb.

MONSIEUR TRITAULT: *(To another visitor:)* Bonjour, madame!

ALICE: Now Monsieur Tritault is going over to greet a very, *very* little old lady in black and she's putting some forget-me-nots in a little blue medicine bottle down by a grave . . . And I'll just get out of their way here . . . *(Alice's footsteps wander along.)* Oh! And along here is a overgrown, neglected corner and . . . here is a semicircle of two . . . three, four, five . . . seven graves about the size of cobblestones. Let's see. This one . . . it's almost covered with moss. *(Reads:)* "Grincheux"—just the name. And the next one is "Simplet." Oh! And the next "Atchoum" . . . Oh, no! *(Translates:)* Sneezy! Oh! And here's one, "Joyeux"—Happy. And "Dormeur"—Sleepy! Oh and then this . . . let's see, "Grincheux" must have been . . . *(Hushed voice:)* it must be Grumpy! Oh, my goodness, and *that* means that this adult-sized grave here, it says, "Son Altesse Royale Princesse Blanche-Neige"! Her Royal Highness Princess Snow White! "Nous n'oublierons jamais"—"We will never forget."

To all you April Fools out there, I'm Alice Furlaud, in Paris.

The Canadian Broadcasting Corporation and Paris Passion *magazine* were the only people insane enough to use this piece. Various producers over the years have accepted it or seriously considered it for April Fool's Day broadcasts, but at the last minute it's always replaced.

My lifelong and brilliant friend Sara Chermayeff has given the piece a certain immortality by loyally playing it over and over on a cassette machine. She maintains it always brings tears to her eyes. Sara is the only person I know who wept at the end of Snow White and the Seven Dwarfs. She was four years old and her mother asked why she was crying all through the happy ending. Sara sobbed, "She never should have left those dwarfs and gone off with that prince!"

The Charge Of The Cow Brigade

It's hard to imagine the Swiss Alps as anything but everlastingly pure and white-topped, with crystal mountain streams, flowery meadows, and innocent cowherds yodelling to each other from Alp to Alp. But even these mountains are beginning to suffer from deforestation, erosion, pollution, and the cause of all three: tourism. An age-old Swiss custom is also threatened—the autumn family ceremony of accompanying the cows, on foot, down from the high summer pastures to the lower pastures before they go into barns for the winter. Every year the cars seem to get more impatient with these little processions , nudging the cows as they sway along with huge bells around their necks; and new roads are making it easier all the time to get the cows down by truck. But when I lived in the Bernese Oberland, the October air was full of bells as the cows came down wearing flowers on their horns, with their owners looking like toys in their cantonal costumes.

One of the families from our village kindly let me spend two of these October days with them: one to get to know the cows, the other to follow them down the mountain, adjusting my tape recorder to the incredibly wild and joyful clanging of their huge bells, keeping my balance and translating what everybody was saying as we scrambled along.

It was a great privilege to be allowed to join in this exhausting ritual. No press person seemed to have thought of reporting on it, so what with the cowbells and yodelling, I managed to make it onto the BBC's early morning program, "Today." The piece started with the ripple of the gentle bells Swiss cows wear in the pasture which, all summer, make the Swiss Alps sound like a giant Hindu temple. These faded down under the following:

HOST: Swiss cows munching musically away in the Alps. They're kept up in the highest pastures all summer while the grass on the lower slopes is grown to make hay. This small herd is about to make the annual autumn descent on foot to their winter quarters. The procession is as sacred a tradition in Switzerland as the numbered bank account. As these cows were being dressed up to go down the mountain, Alice Furlaud prepared to go with them.

ALICE: Marinette Rosat, eleven-year-old daughter of the herd's owners, will be leading the cows down this year, and, of course, she knows all their names—all twenty-four of them.

MARINETTE: Edelweiss, Chamois, Désirée, Miss, Bijou, Hirondelle . . .

ALICE: Marinette is dressed in the local costume of the Pays d'Enhaut—the High Country—between Montreux and Gstaad. She's wearing a striped apron and white stockings, and if it weren't for her Adidas sneakers she'd look just like Heidi. And the scenery—the steep, wooded slopes shining in the autumn sun—it's all like *Heidi* too, except that in Heidi's day this scenery had not yet become the most expensive real estate in the world.

(*Sound: voices, excited thumping, an occasional clang of a deep bell in the cows' section of the Rosat chalet.*)

In the stable before the departure, Marinette's job is to calm the oldest cow, Miss, pronounced *Meese* by Marinette. Miss is butter colored, with a big white face, and she's the queen, or lead cow.

MARINETTE: Hello, Miss. (*Miss: Moo!*)

ALICE: Miss has a gaudy headdress tied to her horns—it's basically an upside-down milking stool covered with pine boughs and homemade paper flowers. Marinette's father and uncles and two little brothers are wearing short-sleeved black velvet jackets. They're all tying the other cows' hats on and strapping huge bells the size of milk buckets onto their necks. (*Clangs, thuds and "allez-allez!" from the men. Then outside, a crowded clanging as cows come out.*)

ALICE: Outside, as the cows are led out, Marinette looks quite frail, with her big stick, facing a fifteen-mile walk down the mountain at the head of these giant cows. She's only eleven years old. But there's nothing frail about her signal to them to get going!

MARINETTE: *(Over the crescendoing clang of bells, mooing, her father's shouts and general chaos)* Hey! Oh yeyyyyy! Viens Miss! Viens Désirée! Yeyyyy! *(Marinette's prolonged cattle call, of a penetrating, galvanizing loudness, was one of the great surprises of the trip. No wonder this eleven-year-old had already won prizes for her yodelling!)*

ALICE: There they go! Here is Chamois, the daughter of Miss, black and white with a fabulous hat. They look like a bunch of ladies going to church. *(We hear the deafening, daunting pagan clang-clang of the huge bells as the cows pick up speed.)* I thought this was going to be a slow and steady procession, but keeping up with the cows as they go down the first steep slopes is quite something. The Rosat family are dashing around with sticks getting these ladies in line . . . *(a few menacing moos)*, and they're really going wild with excitement from the bells, which are meant to be urging them on. They put the bells on the cows for that reason, because the sound excites them. *(Out of breath here. I'm obviously running and dodging cows while trying to make myself heard over bell peals and yelling.)* The same principle as a military procession: soldiers are encouraged by a brass band. . . . It's very narrow here. It's like running before the bulls in Pamplona. Oh, my gosh! *(Pant-pant, clang-clang.)* I've caught up with Monsieur Rosat, head of the family, leading his beautiful black horse with his youngest son Frédéric in the horse cart, all decorated with paper flowers. Ça va vite au début, eh?

MONSIEUR ROSAT: Oui-oui, très vite alors!

ALICE: It goes quickly in the beginning, he's saying.
And down they come. . . . *(Sound all through here: bells of every tone, picking up pace as the slopes grow steeper, nearly drowning out my voice.)*

ALICE: And from this vantage point, those hats are so incredible, really. No Royal Ascot ladies in all their glory were ever arrayed like one of these. And the innkeeper comes out with a bottle of wine and *(huff)* catches up with one of the uncles, and he's quaffing it, and the innkeeper goes on to *(pant)* Monsieur Rosat—and here are some cars—cars, and cows, and everything's getting a bit muddled.

MONSIEUR ROSAT: Ça va aller, ça va aller!

ALICE: Shaking hands with Monsieur Rosat is like having your hand clasped by a giant Brillo pad. And as we arrive down in the valley in Château d'Oex, the village where David Niven lived and died, it's moving to realize that this rough old peasant culture exists side by side with one of the swankiest jet sets on earth. Behind the cuckoo-clock fronts of the old chalets we're passing, live people like Elizabeth Taylor, Julie Andrews and a grand assortment of royal highnesses and billionaires. But this parade of cows with flowered hats is *not* put on for their benefit.

ENGLISH WOMAN: *(From her chalet balcony; she's the downright, middle-aged, bossy type who could easily have played a cameo role in* Jewel in the Crown.*)* The only thing we're sorry about which you *never* used to see before is, you see they've *crossed* the cows. It's because of meat. Meat! It only started about three years ago. Bonjour, Madame! *(Addressing a member of the Rosat family as they and cows clang past:)* C'est bien! C'est bien!

ALICE: Here's Marinette, fresh as a daisy and eating a Mars Bar. Comment ça va, Marinette!

MARINETTE: Ça va, très bien! Un peu mal aux pieds!

ALICE: Her feet hurt a little, she says *(clanging very loud, but slower here)*, and Fifi the dog has come down in a car, and she's joined the procession just for the trip through Château d'Oex to show off, and everybody's leaning out of their windows or on their flowery balconies. The cows are a little bit tired, and they're on their way up to their winter farm, which is a good hour's walk more, uphill this time, from Château d'Oex into the great *(puff)*, green, *(puff-puff)* velvety hills of the Pays d'en Haut.

ALICE: *(Narrating)* The cows have made it home in five hours. On the last steep climb, all the neighbors kept running alongside the herd, handing out glasses of white wine – Swiss white wine, at about four pounds a bottle. The Rosat men drank it down without breaking step. Cousins have appeared in droves for the homecoming party outside the old chalet.

MARINETTE: Yo, do do do lo di, yo do loo loo lo lo, etc. *(An incredible solo performance of yodelling.)*

ALICE: And Marinette, after a whole day of shouting at cows, is still – unbelievably – in good voice.

(*Marinette yodels, then assembled family join in drunken, delighted laughter and whooping.*)

(*Sound: many cowbells, but they sound different—more silvery and melodious, and quieter, because the cows are lying down.*)

ALICE: (*Speaking in the cow pasture over the bells. The parts where cows breathed into or licked the microphone had to be edited out: they sounded like not-very-distant gunfire.*) Out in their home pasture—it's a great green dish in the middle of blue, far-off mountains—the cows are all lying down. They still have their hats on, and they're puffing and blowing a little bit. It's been quite a trip on foot in a country so rich it could easily have afforded to fly each cow down in a separate helicopter. They'll be in this pasture three weeks, then they'll be shut into the barn and they won't see this incredible view again until May, when there's another parade back up to the high pastures.

(*Fade up Marinette and family breaking out in a group yodel accompanied by accordion—a slow, whiffenpoofish, nostalgic song:*) Ya oh, oh oh oh lo lo lo ya-ya-ya di oh!

THE BLUE LOBSTERS OF MONTAUK

Broadcast on "All Things Considered" in 1983.

HOST: Lobsters are very much in the news these days. Medical science is thinking of using their noses to relieve epilepsy, and just the other day one was found off Cape Cod, Massachusetts, who was judged to be 185 years old. Now it is revealed that one out of every thirty million lobsters is bright blue. In a marine laboratory on the tip of Long Island, New York, a biologist has been quietly creating a super-race of these rare lobsters. The genetic research he's doing on them could be the answer to a serious shortage of American lobsters, which have never been scarcer in the coastal shoals or more expensive on restaurant plates. Alice Furlaud went out to Montauk Point to see marine biologist Anthony d'Agostino and his royal family of blue lobsters.

(Sound: hammering and other building noises on Montauk waterfront.)

ALICE: *(Narrating)* The world is trying to beat a pathway to Dr. d'Agostino's door, but it's rough going – through several acres of rubble. The Montauk Blue Lobster Project, in a ramshackle hut on Fort Pond Bay, is all that's left of the former New York Ocean Science Laboratory, which has been demolished by real estate developers to make way for 150 vacation condominiums. *(Sound: lab noises – gurgling and buzzing, etc.)*

ALICE: *(Narrating)* In an age where the world "laboratory" means walls of blinking computers, gleaming glass tubes and white-coated technicians, Dr. d'Agostino and his blue lobsters are carrying on in what appears to be a M*A*S*H unit. Hoses are bubbling air into tanks and fishbowls containing lobsters in various stages of

51

development and various shades of deep, dazzling blue. Dr. d'Agostino, who looks just like Humphrey Bogart with glasses, gave me a lesson in picking up a lobster without getting nipped.

D'AGOSTINO: It will be almost impossible for you to handle without becoming a target.

ALICE: Now you've got a stick between his claws.

D'AGOSTINO: Now what I do is, I give them a target and the target is the stick. That distracts him enough for me to handle him from the rear.

ALICE: Oh, there he comes. Oh!

D'AGOSTINO: And there's the lobster!

ALICE: It's a real Walt Disney cobalt blue!

D'AGOSTINO: Yes. Isn't it spectacular!

ALICE: (*Narrating*) Adult Male number 27 is the translucent blue of sapphires or Gothic cathedral windows. He and his sisters, Emily and Monica, and his brothers, 23 and 17, are the first blue lobsters ever bred in captivity. They're being crossbred to produce the best possible traits for future lobster farming. One of the traits Dr. d'Agostino is breeding for is tameness.

D'AGOSTINO: Now they like being stroked, see?

ALICE: He does look as if he liked being stroked, doesn't he?

D'AGOSTINO: Now it's very calm.

ALICE: That's because he knows you.

D'AGOSTINO: No, it's because they have a nerve right through here which when you rub the exoskeleton essentially acts as a calming, much like you would do to a kitten.

ALICE: Giving a lobster a back rub!

D'AGOSTINO: That's about it! Now you can do that yourself. Just don't put your fingers between the claws.

ALICE: (*Narrating*) All this began ten years ago when a local Montauk lobsterman found a blue lobster in his trap and brought it as a curiosity to Dr. d'Agostino. Through another miracle a blue male was found in Massachusetts, and eventually Dr. d'Agostino discovered that their extraordinary blue color is due to a recessive gene; two blue lobster parents always produce blue offspring—just like blue-eyed people. This meant that blue lobsters were naturally color-coded animals, perfect for studying migration patterns. Better still, another fisherman brought in a superproductive mother lobster called Sophie, whose babies grow at an incredible pace: her descendants often reach the legal size of one pound in three years, while it takes wild lobsters five to seven years to weigh a pound.

D'AGOSTINO: . . . and that particular strain gave us the justification to carry out more breeding experiments to try to sort out this fast-growing trait genetically by old-fashioned breeding crosses. Much like Mendel did with his pea experiment, we are doing the blue-lobster sorting of different traits.

ALICE: Now you breed them: this means you put the males and the females in the same tank at a certain point?

D'AGOSTINO: Well, it's not as simple as that, because during the course of one breeding cycle the female can only mate during the course of six hours out of a whole year! *(Laughs.)*

ALICE: *(Narrating over bubble and glug-glug inside the lab)* And with one blue lobster to every thirty million normal brownish ones, imagine the chances of a female blue lobster meeting a male blue lobster out in the ocean during those crucial six hours—when, being color-blind, they wouldn't even recognize each other! What would they do without Dr. d'Agostino's dating service? Also, in the wild only about a tenth of one percent of lobster eggs survive, whereas Dr. d'Agostino keeps all the lobster eggs he wants. He lifted one of Sophie's pregnant granddaughters out of her tank, with her clutch of 25,000 eggs or so clustered under her tail.

D'AGOSTINO: Oh . . . oh . . . oh . . . don't let me lose the eggs, you yo-yo.

ALICE: Lobster eggs look just like caviar, don't they?

D'AGOSTINO: There are those eggs which sometimes the female drops out of boredom with them.

ALICE: A spontaneous abortion?

D'AGOSTINO: And these are the eggs we use to incubate in those little conicals and then bring through the development stages to the hatch stage. And you see some older specimens, see?

ALICE: It's blue, it's got eyes and it's gambolling around in the bottom of this beaker . . .

D'AGOSTINO: He's having fun because he's eating. We're feeding him miniature brine shrimps. Little tiny shrimps, look how small they are!

ALICE: (*Narrating*) Dr. d'Agostino reckons it will take three years to get a steady, farmable strain of lobsters to pass on to marine farmers. (*Put-put sound of Maine lobster boats.*) Meanwhile in Maine, where the lobsters are supposed to be the tastiest in the world, lobster reinforcements of any color can't arrive too soon. The Maine lobstermen have drastically overfished their waters. I went out in Penobscot Bay with lobsterman Dana Holbrook to see what was in his lobster traps—wooden cages he floats underwater baited with herring.

DANA: Now you always move your trap. No matter if you catch one or no, you move it two, three, four, five feet. Nothin' there so you look for a shoal or a ledge in deep water where they like it. Pay out your warp, make sure your feet aren't caught in it—lose many a fisherman that way. I don't know . . . this lobstering, it's getting worse every year. Too many people in it and fishin' it out too much. Lobsters don't get a chance to reproduce.

ALICE: Now this looks empty, too.

DANA: Yeah, nothin' but a mess of crabs. Mess of crabs, my dear.

ALICE: Now here's a sort of plastic wastebasket—five sleepy or frightened or in-shock lobsters. How many are there, in fact?

DANA: Half a dozen in there, I think, dear. Probably ten pounds or so, forty bucks, so we didn't make a hell of a lot today.

ALICE: (*Narrating; the boat motor goes off in the distance*) With all his problems this year, Dana Holbrook doesn't like to think about the cruel death of lobsters when they're cooked.

DANA: I know one person soaks them in wine. That way they don't feel it. Tough way to go, but they're some good eatin'.

ALICE: *(Narrating; in the background, sounds of the Montauk waterfront, with hammering)* Dr. d'Agostino says he's heard that Montauk blue lobsters taste just as good as any others, but he doesn't know this from experience.

D'AGOSTINO: I have never eaten a blue lobster, although our fishermen have and I do hear about it occasionally. It's natural for me to ask them, "Well, since you cooked one, then what did it taste like?" And they absolutely affirm there's no difference in taste between the blue lobsters versus the mottled brown-colored lobster.

ALICE: You don't eat lobster.

D'AGOSTINO: I certainly cannot eat my experiment!

ALICE: *(Narrating)* It's sad to think of those magical blue creatures who, in older times, would have inspired legends and sagas, being multiplied only to be thrown into boiling water or split open and broiled alive. It's as if all of Mendel's brilliant experiments with peas had been for the benefit of Birdseye. But beware: three years from now, when you're tying on a bib for your shore dinner, you won't know if the lobster on your plate is a Montauk blue or not. When blue lobsters are cooked, their shells turn red.

For National Public Radio, I'm Alice Furlaud, in Montauk, New York. *(I suggested Hoagy Carmichael singing "Am I Blue" to end this piece. I don't know whether NPR found the music or not.)*

PARIS: THE DREAM AND THE AWAKENING

In the month of June 1949, I stepped off the boat train into the Gare St. Lazare, which looked, magically, just like the Monet painting. In the streets, the Paris policemen were behaving like the flirtatious gendarmes of musical comedy. The taxi drivers quoted Voltaire, and students danced round dances on the banks of the Seine. I saw France face to face that summer. Now I see it darkly, through dark filters of small-mindedness (theirs and mine).

It's the same with so many of us expatriates in Paris: we arrive, hearts wide open to experience the dream of France—which, in fact, is also the truth of France—as related to us by literature, children's songs, movies and family. (On my mother's side I come from a long line of raging Francophiles. There has always been an aunt with a niece in tow spending a year in France: my mother, at age fourteen, spent the first year of World War I in Paris, knitting a sock a day for the *poilus*, and later in that war her aunt drove ambulances and did other work for the French wounded. And when my mother's brother was killed in France in 1944, he was buried here, according to the terms of his will—and he was a general in the U.S. Army.)

And for a visit or two, or even a year or two, we do experience that dream. Oh, France, we cannot hold thee close enough, we say, embracing it all: the Seine glinting in the watery afternoon light, the Gardes Republicans clattering by on their horses; a café waiter who reminds us of Jean-Paul Belmondo; a group of pigeons alighting on a snowy roof with the Eiffel Tower in the misty distance; tiny children actually speaking French, the early morning smell of very fresh bread out on the street—we can't get enough of it all! We explore the adorable streets of Paris, hearing imaginary accordion music as we float along—I can hear it right now as I list all these lovely things.

But after a while we begin to shut them out. We close up—shrivelled by sharp tongues, inhospitality, dishonesty in unexpected places, the long, labyrinthine processes required to get things done—the mail forwarded, a decent lease for an apartment, insurance after a fire. We get depressed when salespeople chatter on for minutes—nay, quarters of hours!—with the customer ahead of us—and never give us a glance. In France there is no such concept as "I'll be right with you." Nor is there such a phrase as "Is this seat taken?" as you will find to your cost if you put anything fragile, like a straw hat, on the seat next to you in the Metro. Like Queen Victoria, the French consider it beneath their dignity to look behind them before sitting down. And the prevailing crossness can be wearying. I have days in Paris when everybody—the shopkeepers, the market stall man, the engineer in my recording studio, and the overseas telephone operator—snaps at me in exactly the same tone, as if the whole of Paris had fused into a single, angry personality, determined to berate me.

But I was taken aback one day when Marilyn Robinson of "All Things Considered" said, "The general trend of letters about your pieces is that you're anti-French." Anti-French? Me? Never! Well, I mean, not really. After all, it's only Paris that bears out France's reputation as the home of the rudest people in the world. After Paris, visiting Toulouse, Arras, Strasbourg, Nice, or any other French city is like sinking into a warm bath. And driving through France, following the little roads marked in green on the Michelin map, must be one of the peak travel experiences in the western world. (It's important, though, to do this with the right companion. A trip I once took from Geneva to the Riviera with my Indian guru was a disaster. "This tastes too good. It must have been cooked in meat broth. Tell the waiter to take it away!" he would order.)

So although American residents of Paris do often complain about the French, we also tend to take their side when other Americans criticize them. I always hotly defend the French against the charge that they are grasping materialists only interested in money. A nation of shopkeepers whose motto is obviously "The customer is always wrong," simply cannot care that much about money. And one of my favorite features of life here is that no one is expected to have a beautiful, or even a comfortable, apartment. Mine is furnished largely with rejects found on the street; it's five flights up, with no elevator or central heating. My French friends seem not to notice these deficiencies. They would be amazed at the American custom of asking visitors before they've even been offered a drink, "Would you like to see the house?" and then giving the guest a tour of an unremarkable suburban home, not leaving out a single bathroom or the satin-quilted bedroom of the daughter who is away at college. No French hosts would ever offer such a tour, unless they inhabited the Château de Chenonceaux, and then only after lunch. France is a different kind of consumer society than we are: here they consume delicious food more voraciously than material objects. To put your money in ephemeral things that can be enjoyed here and now—food and drink—seems to me pure wisdom.

The French passion for excellence in eating is still a prime national characteristic, in spite of the new pollution of Paris by restaurants like the Love Burger, the Whataburger, and the Quick, much frequented by the young, perhaps as a revolt against the interminable dinners of their parents. The area that was once the ancient marketplace, Les Halles, has become a blazing neon hell of fast food. But on my street nearby, if you decide on a camembert at the cheese shop, the proprietor asks if you want it ready for lunch or dinner and selects one accordingly.

Recently I overheard two homeless drunks, familiar beggars in my neighborhood, gazing into a pastry-shop window at a gorgeous array of cakes. One of them pointed out, "Celui-là est au Grand Marnier!" ("That one's made with Grand Marnier!") How many American vagrant alcoholics would ever have heard of the liqueur Grand Marnier, or have the chance to spend some of the proceeds of a morning's begging on a cake drenched in the stuff? And outside my local *traiteur*, a glorified caterer-takeout shop, one of which exists in every shopping street in France, every evening there is a line of people. Some of them, I know, share a toilet in the courtyard of their buildings with other tenants. Some are without telephones, many without cars. But they regularly spend large amounts of money on *filet de lièvre façon chasseur, truite en gelée, langouste à la Parisienne,* and other superdelicacies. What brought ordinary French people out on the streets last winter, pummelling striking electrical workers with their fists, was not the cold and dark they had been suffering during weeks of power cuts, but the threat to the quality of French food. The strikes had closed down the bakers' ovens and caused the camembert to ripen at the wrong speed in the cheese shops, so the citizens came out fighting and helped put an end to the strike.

It's this spirit I miss when I am on a long visit to my native U.S.A. With that curse of perpetual homesickness that afflicts so many people who live on both sides of the Atlantic, I miss American friendliness when in France, and when in America I miss the French formality — even if it's only the titles *Madame* and *Monsieur*. I miss the French language frothing around me in the streets, I miss the Paris cafés and I miss my Paris animal friends. Dogs are welcome in restaurants here, and in the post office. Taxi drivers' dogs share the front seat, and the director of the National Archives, a grand palace next door to where I live, used to keep an ancient tortoise in the elegant green courtyard, which it shared, till its death of old age, with a family of black-and-white cats belonging to the gate guard.

The dark side of this prevalence of pets is the cruel French practice of abandoning dogs and cats on the street at vacation time. When Monsieur Jacques Chirac, a dedicated dog lover, was prime minister, I asked him what his government was doing about France's rarely enforceable laws against "l'abandon." He seemed startled: he was holding in his arms a wriggling black Labrador puppy that the Canadian government had just given him, and he had been prepared for the questions Canadian TV reporters were hurling at him about the fishing dispute between Canada and France, but not for one from American radio about stray dogs. I could see from the cold looks of one or two of his staff that, if they could help it, I was never going to be asked back. But Monsieur Chirac answered gamely, if somewhat noncommittally: "We are a country that has the biggest number of dogs per person, which explains this bad phenomenon that we are fighting against, of course."

Like most of my neighbors, I take animals very seriously. Sometimes the dogs and cats of Paris save me from the gloom that fogs the consciousness of so many Parisians. An eager mongrel face will look up at me on the market street where I live, and my vision sharpens. I see the tapestries of vegetables, the mosaics of fresh fish, and down the cross-street, across the river, the top of the central spire of Notre Dame. And the essence and meaning of France, which I felt I had grasped at the Gare St. Lazare on that June day forty years ago, comes back for a moment.

QUAI D'ORSAY ABROAD

*Chinese male opera sopranos appear to be a somewhat endangered
species. Their cause can't have been helped by the Sino-French spy
scandal which inspired the Broadway musical* M. Butterfly.

*By the time NPR assigned me this report, it was too late to track
down the two lovers in the case, one of whom was in jail, the other
in hiding. I had to make do with their lawyer, to whom it was necessary to give the equivalent of Berlitz English Lessons one through
three, before and during the interview. Editing out his "ers" and " 'ow
you say"s was an exercise in invisible mending.*

HOST: *(Susan Stamberg of "All Things Considered")* Now a strange tale
from Europe and the Orient about love and treason, as related to
us by correspondent Alice Furlaud in Paris. It seems that two weeks
ago two men were jailed in that city after one of the most bizarre
trials in French history. The courts decided that Monsieur Bernard
Boursicault, an obscure French diplomat, and his lover, Mr. Shi
Pei Pu, a celebrated soprano at the Peking Opera, had conspired
to pass French secrets to Chinese authorities for fifteen years.

ALICE: And it all happened because Monsieur Boursicault thought
Mr. Shi Pei Pu was a Chinoise, not a Chinois.

HOST: Anyway, Paris is still buzzing with speculation about what
really happened, and Alice Furlaud has her own theories.

ALICE: The French have always relished a nice, sexy spy scandal,
and this one really takes the cake—or, you might say, the fortune
cookie. It all started in 1964 at a reception at the French Embassy
in Peking, where one of the hosts was the embassy accountant, Monsieur Bernard Boursicault, aged twenty, and the guest of honor was

Mr. Shi Pei Pu, star of the Peking Opera, where female roles are performed by men.

(Sound of the high — to western ears — curiously feline singing of Shi Pei Pu. I taped this from a Peking Opera video borrowed from the lawyer. It ran under the following narration:)

ALICE: Now these Chinese opera singers aren't just dressed up with falsies and high heels like the Hasty Pudding Show. They're treated as women by the Chinese public, even off stage. Maître Jacques Peberay, the lawyer who defended Shi Pei Pu:

JACQUES PEBERAY: In the Chinese theater Shi Pei Pu is a woman! A splendid woman!

ALICE: Mr. Shi Pei Pu's most famous role was leading lady in an opera called *The Messenger of Peking*. In this video performance he wears an elaborately embroidered silk gown and looks like the young Merle Oberon at her best. So perhaps it's not surprising that the young diplomat fell madly in love with him. But they didn't actually have an affair until, one day, Shi Pei Pu confided to Monsieur Boursicault that he actually was a woman. And believe it or not, Monsieur Boursicault thought he had a Chinese mistress, just like any normal French diplomat en poste in a foreign land. Not only that, two years later Mr. Shi Pei Pu told Monsieur Boursicault he was pregnant, and soon produced a Eurasian-looking baby called Shi Du Du, whom he brought up with the help of his mother.

Enter one Mr. Kang, of the Chinese secret service, known as The Tiger. Kang threatened to have the authorities separate the lovers if Monsieur Boursicault didn't hand over any information he had access to about the Russians. So Monsieur Boursicault began ransacking the embassy files for secrets, which he regularly gave to Mr. Kang, and the love affair continued for nearly twenty years.

In 1980, Monsieur Boursicault was sent back to Paris, and shortly afterwards Shi Pei Pu, now in his forties, came to Paris on a cultural exchange program. He and his son went to live with Monsieur Boursicault on the Boulevard Raspail.

And now Mr. Shi informed Monsieur Boursicault that he was a man after all! But to the French counter-espionage service, who had finally noticed the couple, it was "Cherchez la femme" as usual. They thought that Shi Pei Pu was a woman and a mother for two whole years — only catching on just before the trial, at which the two men appeared side by side in dark blue pin-striped suits. Paris gossips seem to feel Monsieur Boursicault deserves his sentence. But some of them are asking why Mr. Shi Pei Pu should get six years in jail if, as his lawyer says, he did not actually handle a single document. And how—physically how—everybody's saying, did Shi Pei Pu contrive all those years to make this Frenchman think it was "Vive la différence" when it was really "Vive la Même chose"? Defense lawyer Jacques Peberay puts it all down to inexperience:

JACQUES PEBERAY: Boursicault and Shi Pei Pu are virgins at that time. And—*comment est-ce qu'on dit très naif?*

ALICE: And very naive!

JACQUES PEBERAY: And very naifs—comment dit-on sexe *organe?*

ALICE: That's perfect: sex organ.

JACQUES PEBERAY: Sex organs, they are very, very, very little.

ALICE: (*Interrupting quickly in the studio*) Apart from this, Monsieur Peberay is a bit vague.

But the real mystery of the mysterious East is how Mr. Shi Pei Pu made Monsieur Boursicault believe he'd had that baby. According to Monsieur Peberay, Shi Pei Pu kept collecting Monsieur Boursicault's semen and had a doctor implant it into a woman, who gave birth to Shi Du Du and disappeared from the scene. Only three out of seven judges in the Court of Assizes believed this tale. And indeed, some Parisians are saying that with Monsieur Peberay as a defense lawyer, who needs the prosecution?

But Peberay is deeply sympathetic with his client's sad situation. He's vowed to get him out of prison somehow. He's organizing a personal appeal to President Mitterand for mercy. Mitterand has long been known to the French public as "The Sphinx," the classic solver of riddles. Maybe he can figure it all out. For National Public Radio, I'm Alice Furlaud, in Paris. Wait, wait! I forgot to tell you some important details! It was on a chance visit to the family doctor, Dr. Ma, that Shi Pei Pu found out he wasn't a woman. And I didn't tell you where Shi Du Du was! She, I mean he, is with his mother, I mean his father, I mean they're both in prison and they're both men, and now we hear they don't even love each other any more, and . . . (*Fades down and out, spluttering.*)

BOYS IN THE WOOD

It is an accident that two of the broadcasts I have done in an embar-
rassingly short career were about transvestites. When I began to track
down Mark Turlock, the very shy author of this guide to prostitution
in the Bois de Boulogne, I had no idea the prostitutes would be any
different than those who had prowled the Bois since the Belle Epoque.
It was a surprise that most of them were Brazilian men. The piece
aired in 1979.

ALICE: *(Narrating)* The Bois de Boulogne, that great wooded park
on the west side of Paris, has long been famous for its ladies of the
evening. In surprising numbers, they stand openly along the miles
of roads curving through the eight square kilometers of forest, wearing
practically nothing. Right now, with summer at its height, this very
French outdoor activity is flourishing. Just in time for the tourist
trade, a guide has come out called *A Sexual Tour of the Bois de
Boulogne*. It costs thirty-nine francs, about five dollars, and it is the
talk of the town. It's been done with the careful detail of a military
ordnance survey map: colored squares and numbers mark the exact
location of the various sexual attractions on offer in the Bois. On
the edges of the map are descriptions of the precise hours, prices,
and what to expect, in both French and English. Japanese is going
to be added in the next edition. The author of this indispensable
work is Mark Turlock, a thirty-five-year-old French disc jockey at
a respectable Paris radio station. He makes it clear that his research
was original.

MARK: Always I have lived around the wood, you know? And I was
obliged to cross the wood every day during ten years. And I see

63

the people in the wood—sex people in the wood, and I try to know more what happens in the wood at night.

ALICE: *(Narrating)* Calling the Bois de Boulogne "the wood" makes it sound so innocent—just about as innocent as Little Red Riding Hood in Perrault's insinuating original version. And the tone of the guide is innocent and serious. An example from the transvestite section, I quote: "There are two principal nationalities of transvestite in the Bois: the French, indicated by a red *F* on the map, and the Brazilian, indicated by a red *B*." According to the guide, the Brazilians are in the majority. Transvestites are men who like to dress as women, and they have existed at least since that wolf dressed up as Little Red Riding Hood's grandmother. Thanks to modern medicine, some of the ones in the Bois are not only made up as women, but made *into* women. They can earn around a thousand dollars in one month, and they have wiped the old-fashioned Irma La Douces, who traditionally sold their favors in the Bois, off the map.

MARK: The news is this: homosexuals go with homosexuals, and the new type of men, not homosexual, like to be with transvestites. When the man meets the transvestite, he is going with a girl with a male sex, and not with a man with the breasts of a girl, you know? I mean this is very new!

ALICE: It sounds incredibly new!

MARK: It is the only place in the world like this where you have all this kind of sex. This is very important: transvestites, partouses [multiple-partner parties], exhibitionists, homosexuals, prostitute men, prostitute girls, only in this place you have, only in Bois de Boulogne. You must come; it's very nice.

ALICE: Everyone would not agree with map maker Mark Turlock on this point. But his invitation to drive past some of the places on the map was accepted.

MARK: Now we go on the Route des Lacs in Passy, between Lake Inferior and Lake Superior. Hop! Take my car, and go! *(Sound of car starting, vroom-vrooming, then stopping.)* I'll look to see if I haven't got transvestites under my car, because they like very much this.

ALICE: They go under the cars when the police come?

MARK: Yeah. There are no transvestites there, I know now. *(Car starts.)*

ALICE: *(Over sounds of car motor as Mark maneuvers it through Bois)* There are so many cars, I'm amazed. You think of the Bois de Boulogne as being all green and leafy, and a paradise of nature; in fact, everything seems to be done in cars. There's no way you can get away from the sound of cars, and all these different activities take place in or around cars. But the transvestites are outside on the park benches and you pick them up: you drive slowly by them and look to see which one you like best, and . . .

MARK: *(Interrupts)* Look! Look! All the cars are cruising now. And during all the night it's like this: sometimes you cannot drive, you know? It's impossible!

ALICE: Traffic jam of people looking for transvestites!

MARK: Yeah. It's terrible! Now we are here: I show you on the map, eh? We are here—Cascade. It's a very nice restaurant.

ALICE: Cascade meaning waterfall, and it's all lit up . . .

MARK: You see? On your right. She is not nude, eh? I say "she," but it's a he, a man. She's not nude, but she's beginning to work, eh? She's beautiful.

ALICE: *(Trying a little breathlessly to get into the spirit of the thing)* Very beautiful. Very chic. She looks as if she's dressed by Yves St. Laurent.

MARK: Yes, but it is a man, eh? Don't forget this. It's not a girl.

ALICE: Now here's a taxi arriving with a really fabulous-looking girl, who is a man. And—do you think she's Brazilian?

MARK: I am sure, yeah. All this part is the area of Brazil people, you know? Here we arrive to a very special place, it's for voyeurism. Exhibitionism, you know?

ALICE: Now let's see where this is on the map. The voyeur section is to the west of the lake, right? *(Mark murmurs assent.)* OK, let's read from the map: "This is the most exciting sport that you'll ever see at night in the Bois. The thing is to catch high-class women who exhibit themselves, sometimes with their husbands, and also make love with unknowns. She may even bring one or more men to her home. In any case, be patient, discreet, and polite. P.S. Don't forget your flashlight."

MARK: Yes, because sometimes it's dark, and to see the girl in the car you must have your flashlight, you know?

ALICE: If you're going to be a voyeur, you have to be able to see.

MARK: Of course.

ALICE: *(Narrating)* One wonders what motivated Mark Turlock to spend several years compiling this detailed guidebook. Apparently he believes that this squalid side of outdoor Paris is an important French institution.

MARK: It's a place like Tour Eiffel, like Louvre, like Arc de Triomphe, like Folies Bergères, and it's less expensive than Folies Bergères. The Bois de Boulogne is an exceptional place.

ALICE: *(Narrating)* The French police do not share Mark's respect for the goings-on in the Bois. For years they've been lenient about prostitution, but with so many foreign men getting into the act, the police have announced that they're going to crack down. So any unwary curiosity seeker who ventures into the Bois de Boulogne this summer should be warned: the pretty girl in the topless tutu behind the tree might turn out to be not a Brazilian boy, but a French gendarme. For National Public Radio, this is your den mother of iniquity, Alice Furlaud, in Paris.

I was the only "media" person to drive through the Bois with this odd young man. Maybe my cozy old middle-aged appearance reassured him. I hope not. But toward the end of the trip, he clearly regretted having brought even me. I've never known why. He refused to stop and let me talk to any of the sylvan transvestites. He said gloomily that he had turned everybody down, even BBC television, that this was the last time he would deal with the press, and could he drop me at a bus stop.

This was one of the first features I ever did for the radio, and I found that managing the tape recorder, peering at male prostitutes, and asking the right questions all at once was nearly too much for me. I kept talking nervously into the microphone, giving a running commentary on the proceedings, perhaps influenced by childhood memories of war time, Elmer-Davis-visits-the-troops style radio, or by the horse races which my father listened to on Saturdays. This is not, I later found, correct practice except in emergencies like war. Most people tape the interviewees' comments as well as a lot of whatever sound is in the background. At the studio, you run this ambience under your narration; you're not supposed to pretend to be out in the field exactly, but it gives the script a little atmosphere.

In this case, my sports-announcer treatment worked. While visiting friends in Toronto that summer, I took the piece to the Canadian Broadcasting Corporation and played it as a sample of my work, to a tremendously august person, producer of a revered weekly three-hour magazine program called "Sunday Morning." He asked suspiciously, but with a certain admiration, if I had really ad-libbed all that stuff out in the Bois. He said, sourly, that he would be glad to have me on "Sunday Morning," but never with a feature on such a distasteful subject.

"All Things Considered" loved it, though. My first visit to National Public Radio in Washington was illuminated by host Susan Stamberg and other friendly people greeting me with joyful cries of "Alice! Miss Moral Turpitude 1979!" and the like. It seemed a little thing to make a fuss about: after all, I'd created a seven-minute feature, not the Kinsey Report. But my new friends happily brandished the hate mail the piece had inspired. One man—an elderly-sounding type from an elderly-sounding Boston law firm—wrote that he had contributed generously to NPR since it began, but that now he'd heard this tasteless and shocking report, he was never going to give them another cent. It is typical of the disinterested purity of the NPR crowd that these furious letters enhanced my position there at a time when, due to the over-expansive activities of its former chief, Frank Manckiewicz, the network was desperately in the red and close to capsizing altogether.

WINDSORS IN THE WOOD

One of the landmarks pointed out to me by that chronicler of voyeurs and transvestites in the Bois de Boulogne was a stately white villa, standing rather mournfully back from the road behind its gate house. It belonged to the former King of England, the Duke of Windsor. He had died seven years before and the Duchess was in the house, dying, it was said.

Back in the early 1970s I'd been amazed when our friend Kathy, a twenty-six-year-old college graduate, wise in the ways of yoga, meditation and awareness, said she had never heard of the Duke of Windsor, or even of his abdication in 1936 to marry a twice-divorced American. Kathy laughed at me for knowing these things, in the same gently scornful way I have laughed at snobbish Americans who know all about deposed European royalty and can tell the Bourbon-Parmes from the Bourbon-Siciles and I don't know who all. I thought of asking Kathy if she'd ever heard of the Second World War. Her scorn stung me. My generation was brought up hearing the word "Mrs. Simpson" as a synonym for wicked and worldly. This attitude was perhaps more concentrated in Baltimore, where I was born. I remember my mother describing the reception at the Elk Ridge Kennel Club for the Duke and Duchess on their first visit to the Duchess's native Baltimore, where all the women who had spoken despisingly of the former Wallis Warfield for seducing the king, flocked to curtsy to her. As a girl my mother had swooned over the Duke, then Prince of Wales, when he visited her Washington boarding school and declared that day a holiday. But a friend of hers had been to school with the Duchess and described her as "fast," an adjective which stuck to her in my mind.

In fact, my husband, Max, is the only person I know who has nothing but good to say of the Duchess. He met her in Lisbon in 1940, when the Duke and Duchess and Max, aged fifteen, were escaping from German-occupied France. At meals at the American Legation, where Max and his family were staying, the Duchess went out of her way to be charming to him and he was entranced. He couldn't, however, see what she saw in the former King of England.

I once saw the Duke and Duchess of Windsor at a dance in New York—a tiny couple, very straight-backed, like figures on a wedding cake, only both were in black. I remember my "aha!" experience at the sight of the Duke's perfect-fitting dress suit. Until then all black, tuxedolike garments—whether worn by waiters, orchestra musicians, magicians, my father, or the boys who did or didn't cut in on me— had looked more or less alike. Now I realized there could be a huge quantum leap of a difference.

Many years later I saw that same beautifully tailored tuxedo along with several others, when I interviewed the valet who had pressed it for the dance. Mr. Mohammed al-Fayed, the Egyptian tycoon, had moved into the ducal house in the Bois and was creating there a museum in memory of the Windsors. I was assigned to the story by Dona Guimaraes, editor of the "Home" section of the New York Times, who thrilled me by putting it on the front page of the section on Christmas day, under a story about another royal family, that of Babar the Elephant.

A few months and a few stories earlier, on my first visit to that vast expanse of wall-less offices which is the New York Times, I had actually met Dona. She stood out—or rather sat at her computer— like the dark, intense, glamorous headmistress of some aristocratic school. She wore a heavy white sweater such as one might borrow from a football-playing boyfriend—but with a beautiful crystal necklace. It was a fashion statement which pronounced my careful little black suit a failure.

The editing, consisting at my end of a series of harrowing transatlantic telephone calls (How much rent did they pay? What brand of bath salts? Write a paragraph on that and call back in twenty minutes!) was done on Christmas Eve. I was allowed to run out at about seven and buy a few things for next day's Christmas dinner, but by eleven the apartment was still cold, filthy and littered with rejected manuscript pages. When Dona says, "It's a wonderful story," you go leaping and skipping around the room, chanting a joyful tune to yourself.

69

But Dona never gives a hint that she might speak this line until the story is completely finished. Until then it's the relationship of the private to the regimental sergeant-major—terrifying. But there was one lovely moment during the agonizing editing process. I had put on one side as an alternative paragraph a section I'd written about a Holbein portrait of a royal child, picked by the Duke from Hampton Court to accompany him in his exile. At one point in the tense negotiations, I said, "We could always put in the part about the royal baby." A shout from Dona came down the line: "What royal baby?!"

Here's the version I did for BBC's "Woman's Hour":

(Ambience: birds tweet over distant traffic. Sound fades under narration.)

ALICE: This graceful nineteenth-century villa, with its white columns and landscaped lawns, looks just the place to take a rest from being royalty. The nearest houses here on the edge of the woods once belonged to rich Parisians. Now they're institutions belonging to the City of Paris, which also owns this house. Since 1953, the city has rented it to the Duke and Duchess of Windsor for a nominal rent thought to be about thirty-five pounds a year. Now that the couple is dead, the city is leasing it to Mr. Mohammed al-Fayed for fifty years, also for practically nothing, with the understanding that he'll keep the place up in grand style. Mr. al-Fayed was made a Knight of the Legion of Honor by President Mitterand for restoring the Paris Ritz hotel, another piece of romantic real estate he owns, along with Harrods. So in London I asked him why he wants to take on a Windsor museum, too. He told me that being a native of Alexandria, Egypt, he's always been fascinated by the romantic aspects of history.

MOHAMMED AL-FAYED: And if you grow up with this fascination of a great civilization you know, especially a city like Alexandria, which is the most romantic city—Antonio fell in love with Cleopatra there, didn't he?

ALICE: *(Narrating)* The idea of Edward VIII's sacrifice of power obviously moves Mr. al-Fayed.

MOHAMMED AL-FAYED: How can a great king of a great empire just renounce everything and say goodbye, for the love of a woman? Just go! For the love of a woman! It's unbelievable!

EDWARD VIII SPEECH: You must believe me when I tell you that I have found it impossible to carry the heavy burden of responsibility and to discharge my duties as king as I would wish to do, without the help and support of the woman I love. And I want you to know . . .

ALICE: *(Narrating)* But not everybody who admires a historic figure would want to live in his house with all his personal possessions, right down to the last pair of suspenders. Mr. al-Fayed stepped in last summer and bought the entire contents of the Windsors' house just as they were about to be auctioned off: he says he'll spend about two million pounds to convert the third floor into an apartment for himself and his family; the other rooms will be kept as the Windsors lived in them. He has offered the Queen of England her pick of the furnishings, including the small leather-topped table on which Edward VIII signed his abdication in 1936. It is not known if the queen will *want* to own a piece of furniture associated with abdication. But probably the greatest treasure of all the Windsor memorabilia in the house is Sidney Johnson, a sixty-three-year-old Bahamian who, for many years, was the Duke of Windsor's valet.

MOHAMMED AL-FAYED: He joined the Duke when he was governor of the Bahamas, as a little boy fifteen years old, and stayed with him for thirty-five years as his own personal valet, with him every day and night, travelling everywhere. He is a dictionary of everything, you know? A very cultured man.

(Sound of Sidney's footsteps coming down long marble staircase in the house fades under.)

ALICE: *(Narrating)* Sidney Johnson has been installed in the Paris house as Mr. al-Fayed's valet and a kind of curator. A tour with him around this fourteen-room miniature château, all full of the glitter and gold of mirrors and chandeliers and ormolu, ought to be a boon to historians. They're the only people besides the British royal family who'll be allowed to visit the museum.

SIDNEY JOHNSON: This is the boudoir: they used to have dinner here alone. We'd put these two tables here, like the table you had tea on downstairs?, and they'd have their dinner here with their little dogs around them, and they'd have a little drink or something like that—they would talk and have a little Scotch. They'd finish

71

by nine o'clock, and at ten o'clock I'd take the dogs downstairs and she'd say, "Goodnight, Sidney," and they'd sit here and talk. This was their boudoir.

ALICE: *(Narrating)* It was Sidney Johnson who put the Windsors' possessions back in their right places: the embroidered linen sheets, and the photographs of royal relations signed with nicknames, and the portraits of pug dogs. He knows all the history of everything here, from the eighteenth-century Chinese wallpaper to the needlepoint cushions.

SIDNEY JOHNSON: His mother taught him how to do this.

ALICE: She taught him how to do needlepoint?

SIDNEY JOHNSON: Yes, he used to knit socks and things for the Red Cross in the Bahamas—scarves and everything—in his spare time.

ALICE: *(Narrating)* It sounds as if the Duke and Duchess of Windsor had lots of spare time. But Sidney Johnson remembers that the famous parties they gave required a lot of hard work.

SIDNEY JOHNSON: And after the hairdresser had done her hair, she'd come down in one of these toweling dressing gowns, she'd stand over there, touch everything on the table, check everything, look at the glasses, look at the cards if they were in the correct places, the flowers—she checked everything beforehand. This was her life. She was a great hostess, no doubt about that.

ALICE: *(Narrating)* And the basement kitchens where these grand dinners were cooked, are vast.

SIDNEY JOHNSON: This is where they did all the pastry and the croissants, and all that kind of thing.

ALICE: Croissants specially made for them? Ohhhh! *(Envious quaver.)* You know, when they talk about giving up everything for the woman you love, what did they really give up?

SIDNEY JOHNSON: *(Laughs with his special young and delighted kind of laugh)* There was a pastry cook, the chef, the one who did the vegetables, and there was a man—there were four in the kitchen all day long. Yeah! The Duchess loved her food. She didn't eat much, but she wanted her friends to enjoy her cooking.

ALICE: She said "you can never be too rich. . . ."

SIDNEY JOHNSON: ". . . or too thin," that's right! But there were times when she was living on a carrot and a cup of tea. That's what ruined her. She dieted too much. Especially in collection times. She would get up in the morning and just taste a cup of tea and she was out at the dress collections all day. I don't know where she got the strength to do what she did.

ALICE: (*Narrating*) Upstairs in the dressing rooms, Sidney Johnson has put the ducal clothes, beautifully pressed, back in the ducal closets and drawers.

SIDNEY JOHNSON: These are all the kilt socks.

ALICE: Oh, the socks that match the kilts! (*Thumping of drawers being opened and shut is heard in background.*)

SIDNEY JOHNSON: Every suit was numbered. The evening suits were numbered. And I had to remember whether it was number one, two, three, four, or five.

ALICE: Of his evening clothes? Why would they need to be numbered?

SIDNEY JOHNSON: Because he doesn't want to wear the same one every day! Now his day clothes, if it's summertime I'll give him what I want, if it's a town suit I give him what I want. But evening suits, never mind, they had to be number one, number two, number three, number four. But there's one little one that I can't seem—I'm still looking for it. It's a blue one with white stripes, he called it his "thinking coat." When he was working—when he was writing his book, when he was doing his stocks and shares, he was wearing this coat.

ALICE: (*Narrating*) Mr. Johnson was with the Duke when he died.

SIDNEY JOHNSON: He got up that morning and he said to me, "Sidney, I feel like writing some letters. I want to write some letters, so would you take me up?" I said, "Yes, of course." I got him up, sat him at his desk, gave him his pen, and he said to me, "Sidney, it's a funny thing, I can't even move my pen!" I said, "How could you? You haven't eaten anything for a month!" I said, "You're too weak, you must eat!" and I said, "You always like your Finnan haddock and some scrambled eggs; why don't you let me go down and get them for you?" He said, "Sidney, all that is in the past." He said, "I don't feel like that." He said, "I tell you what! I feel like having some peaches and cream." I said, "Fine! That's something!" He said, "How long will it take?" I said, "Five minutes." I went down to the kitchen, I came up, he said, "That was quick!" I set it on his desk, and he started to take the spoon. But he couldn't get it to his mouth. He said, "Sidney, look! look! I can't. . . ." I said, "Let me feed you. Do you mind?" Because he was such a proud man, you'd have to be careful. He'd say, "What are you talking about: a baby?" So he said, "Yes, do it." So he had four peaches, four whole peaches and the cream. He said, "I feel rather tired now. I feel like going to bed." He said, "Draw the blinds." So I did, and he said, "Don't wake me. Keep the dog out." And the dog didn't come in any more. He just jumped off his bed and left, and went into the boudoir of the Duchess and never came back. I thought that was a very funny thing. That same night, it was the end. He died.

ALICE: (*Narrating*) There are men, it seems, who are heroes to their valets. And now Sidney Johnson will be back in his old home, tying the ties of Mohammed al-Fayed—maybe even in Windsor knots. And he sounds delighted.

SIDNEY JOHNSON: Mr. Fayed is the most wonderful person, he loves history, he loves old things. And I am so happy, ma'am, that he got this place, and it brings back old memories to me. Luckily he came here, he got all these things, because if it had gone on sale the whole of this place would have been sold everywhere. And no one would have known where his Royal Highness's things went.

I remember standing in the crumbling, echoing basement kitchen at Le Bois with Sidney Johnson, and two maids and a chauffeur who were still on duty, waiting to see what use Mr. al-Fayed would make of them. In low tones they spoke to each other of the Duchess's suffering in her long last illness; the old friends who never came to see her, the few who did come; the stray cats the Duchess used to feed every day at the edge of the garden where the dark forest began. The maids were still feeding the cats. I had spent two long winter afternoons in the house with the elegant, nimble-minded, kindly Sidney Johnson, who devoted to my article an eager energy he could have used to great advantage in a book of his own—a book he had volunteered never to write.

He had given me just the right glimpses into Windsor-land: the dining-room curtains which Prince Charles, while having lunch with Mr. al-Fayed at Le Bois, had recognized from several visits he had made to his great-uncle; Sidney noted that Mr. al-Fayed had had these curtains turned upside down: the hems had been spoiled by the dogs "lifting their legs on them for years." There was the cushion on which the Duke's mother, Queen Mary, had cross-stitched "What is Home Without Pleasure?" The Duke, Sidney said, had never stopped missing his mother. Most touching, most haunting of all, he had shown me all those closets of the Duke's shoes, kilts, etc.

Late that night I realized with a shock that the concentration needed for taping Sidney's answers at the right sound level had cut me off from awareness of the true situation. I had been in the private dressing room not of the disgraced, frivolous king I'd read about in so many magazines, but of a frail old man who had carefully cherished his ancient tweeds, and who, if alive, would have been astonished and horrified to find me there. Never mind that every one of the Duke of Windsor's plaid-topped socks, Turnbull and Asser shirts and black silk ties now belonged to an Egyptian billionaire. Those beautiful English clothes should have been burned before they were defiled by me and my tape recorder.

I did not, however, fail to describe them to the readers of the "Home" section of the New York Times.

I telephoned Sidney the other day. He told me the house is still in the process of restoration. The maids, Victoria and Maria, and the chauffeur, Martin, are still in the employ of Mr. al-Fayed, whose wife is "cat crazy" and has seen to it that all the stray cats they could catch have found homes. As to those other denizens of the Bois de Boulogne, the male prostitutes, I don't know what effect, if any, AIDS has had on them.

From the distance of two years, I see them all—Brazilians, cats, and the late Windsors—as the beyond-the-pale residents of the Bois, as opposed to the exclusive clubs, grand restaurants, nannies and up-market children in the Bois who are safely inside the epistemological structure of reality we all pretend to accept. If you are a prostitute, say the rules, you should be a prostitute of the sex which God gave you. If you're a king, you don't abandon your throne, especially not for a divorcée from Baltimore. And if you're a homeless cat, you are so unimportant that it's sinfully frivolous even to mention you.

But it's all beginning to shift. The good-guy structure of science, which denies the existence of the subjective and therefore the existence of people as they actually are, is being smashed by stampeding atoms and viruses from beyond the pale. And in the case of AIDS, it may well be the beyond-the-pale Duchess who saves the day, benefiting AIDS victims and cats alike. The Duchess of Windsor left all the vast wealth she inherited from her regal husband—some $45 million—to France's Pasteur Institute for research. She stipulated that none of the money should be used for experiments on animals.

THE CATS OF PARIS

The Paris cats supported by the Duchess of Windsor in the Bois de Boulogne were the lucky ones. The lives of homeless Paris cats get sadder and more perilous every day as traffic increases and quiet nooks, crannies and old ladies decrease. My feature on this subject for the BBC was repeated twice, which made me purr with satisfaction.

HOST: France has the largest number of pet owners of any European country. Fifty-two percent of all French families keep some sort of pet, and there are an estimated seven million cats in France. Not all of these cats are happy cats, and who knows better than Paris resident Alice Furlaud, who helps feed a colony of abandoned cats near the Paris church of St. Gervais—an activity forbidden by the police.

(Sound of the bells of St. Gervais over me muttering about cats and trying to manage microphone, tape recorder and cat food all at once.)

ALICE: OK. I've got a can of condensed milk, and I'm doing this in secret. There's the big grey ruffly cat—beautiful. There's the slightly thinner brown-and-grey one. Where's the black, lame one? Wait! I'm going to get my milk out. *(Sound of purring while eating.)*

ALICE: *(Narrating)* The opulent tiger-and-white cat, Apollinaire, was once a homeless cat, too: now he lives in a grand apartment in Versailles, and his diet is very different from that of the poor outdoor cats, according to his owner, fifteen-year-old Sebastien Huite.

SEBASTIEN: With his paw he can open the fridge very easily, so now we have to put a string so that he can't open it, because he eats everything inside. *(Sound of Apollinaire purring—a rich, masculine purr—runs under next script.)*

ALICE: (*Narrating*) Paris cats Rousski and Kalinka do not get to raid the icebox, but their owner, Anne-Marie Thibault, serves them a balanced diet à la française, with meat and assorted vegetables.

ANNE-MARIE: I cook up a big plate: pussycat casserole. They do like the meat better, I must admit, and they have trouble eating the peas, because they roll.

(*Sound of purring, this time Rousski.*)

ALICE: (*Narrating*) Rousski and Kalinka both have identification numbers tattooed in one ear. The numbers are registered at a Feline Center—there's also a Canine Center—and the system is said to have brought lots of lost cats and dogs back to their owners. (*More Rousski purring.*)

ALICE: OK, Kitty, let's look in your ear and see the tattoo.

ANNE-MARIE: The tattoo is always in the right ear, it is in blue.

ALICE: Let me see if I can read that. It's—oh, wait, it's going to be difficult for the person who finds this kitty. I can read A, Z, 474, and another funny letter in the back which looks like Q. What does it look like to you?

ANNE-MARIE: Nine!

(*Sound: a sad cat howls from his basket at the animal assistance shelter; despairing barks are also heard under the next bit of narration.*)

ALICE: (*Narrating*) Rousski and Kalinka had their ears tattooed at the Paris animal shelter, Assistance Aux Animaux—Assistance to Animals—where Anne-Marie originally found them. On a recent Saturday the waiting room was full of cats and dogs in or out of baskets, waiting to be tattooed or spayed—free of charge for the needier cases. Natalie, who was on duty that morning, showed me the twenty cats in cages who are up for adoption. One was twelve years old, one eight—their mistresses had died—and one, a white one, was blind. Natalie has great hopes that homes will be found for all of them.

NATALIE: Ah oui, tous! (Yes, all of them!) Même si on a un certain temps pour les placer. (Even if it takes quite a while to place them.)

ALICE: *(Narrating)* So many of the cats I meet in Paris have been taken in because somebody else threw them out. In a rough and tough café on the Rue Rambuteau lives Clémentine, a smoky grey cat who was found three years ago by one of the café's customers in the cemetery of Montmartre. The daughter of the house, Cristelle, told me Clémentine was still very shy and likely to bite.

CRISTELLE: *(A piping, high, eight-year-old voice)* Elle n'aime pas qu'on la caresse.

ALICE: Pourquoi?

CRISTELLE: Quand elle en a mare elle nous mord!

(Sound of pinball machines under following narration:)

ALICE: It's no wonder Clémentine is so very wary, what with all the noise from the pinball machines, or *flippaires*. In fact, while the stray-cat population of Paris keeps increasing, the number of contented cats belonging to Paris cafés and shops and restaurants seems to be to be dwindling—drastically. Mademoiselle Georgette, who owned the newspaper store on the Ile St. Louis, with a fat cat asleep on every pile of magazines, has retired and taken her cats home with her. Cha-Cha, my baker's cat with the floury whiskers, disappeared forever one day, and so did the pharmacy cat who used to lie in the window in a bowl of tea leaves: my neighbors suspect the local Chinese restaurant. The truth is that the old, central part of Paris, with its lethal traffic, its cafés vibrating with video games, and its original population being chased out into the suburbs by high rents, is no longer a good environment for cats. But there are still lots of people with the special love and respect Parisians have for what they call *chats de gouttière*—cats of the gutter. But they're cats of the gutters of Paris, remember, and they've been loved by people like Montaigne, and Alexandre Dumas and Victor Hugo—and the powerful seventeenth-century Cardinal Richelieu, who once gave a friend's cat a munificent state pension.

(Sound: a montage of different purring sounds, then:)

ALICE: *(At church of St. Gervais)* There's the lame one! Minou! Minou! Oh, good, the lame one is finally getting something! *(Purring fades out.)*

PET FOOD U.S.A.

My first and last experience of eating cat food and dog food took place on "All Things Considered" circa 1985. It all started in a supermarket in Massachusetts.

(Sound: the rough and tumble sounds of an American supermarket fade under.)

ALICE: *(Narrating)* Simmered Beef Dinner, Chopped Grill, Fisherman's Stew, Poached Salmon Dinner, Cape Cod-Style Platter, Braised Liver Entrée, Beef-Basted Waffles; *not* items on a restaurant menu, but labels on cans of cat food. The last time I shopped for my mother's cat, the names were strictly feline: Puss-in-Boots, Felix, Nine Lives: but now there's a definite trend toward human recipe names. Some give a French cuisine image: Buffet, Chef's Blend, Gourmet Platter. And cheese is a new pet food ingredient: Beef and Cheese in Sauce, Choice Cuts 'n Cheese, Chicken and Cheese Dinner. My mother's cat rather likes Fancy Feast, in tiny cans that are self-opening, like beer. Not that cats can open these cans themselves: that will probably be next year's humanoid pet-food surprise.

Is all this meant to convince the cat's owner that at two cans for sixty-nine cents he's buying his cat the same food *he* eats? No one who's eaten a spoonful of Super Supper, as I have, would believe that.

The new dog food titles are less pretentious—more masculine, but still different from the classic Pal and Ken'l Ration I remember. There's Come 'N' Get It, Ranch Supper, Mighty Dog and a new taste breakthrough called Wagtime.

There's a simpler pet-food section in my local supermarket, or *supermarché*, in Paris. For dogs there's basically Canigou or Loyal;

for cats there's Kitekat, Whiskas, and Ron-ron (that's French for purring). The only reference here to human haute cuisine is rabbit mousse—a sadly cannibalistic cat food. I mean, you wouldn't feed a cat to a rabbit, so why feed a rabbit to a cat?

People are supposed to eat pet food during economic depressions. I don't believe it. Any sensible pauper would be a vegetarian rather than eat Fish Ahoy or Hearty Stew. In New York City I had dinner with a tiny, cinnamon-colored poodle called Eddie. *(Eddie barks and barks and barks.)* We carefully read the label on the can beforehand.

ALICE: *(In Eddie's apartment)* "Mighty Dog meets or exceeds the minimum nutritional levels for all stages of your dog's life." Do you hear that, Eddie? ". . . as established by the National Research Council of the National Academy of Sciences." It's got beef, chicken, water, seasoning, salt and onion powder, minerals and vitamins, potassium chloride. It says it's "specially balanced and fortified to provide a hundred percent of your dog's daily nutritional needs." OK, we're going to have some. Both of us are going to have a little bite, Eddie. Eddie's going to have his first. Here! He doesn't seem to like it tonight. Come on, Eddie, here it is. OK, I'm going to take my teaspoonful first. Hmmmm. It's really—oh, no! Ergh! At first it tastes a little bit like any ordinary potted meat, but there's a sort of bad, slightly rotten taste to it. It isn't all that—ugh!

The fact is, most pet food is just slaughterhouse leftovers: ground-up innards and, for all I know, whiskers, teeth, beaks, eyes—in a word, offal. And it *is* awful. Of course, hungry people in famine areas would be glad of it. But as long as we in the affluent West do keep our fellow animals as pets, and as long as we ourselves eat so much meat, I wonder: why should we serve pets this inferior food under these human-quality-sounding titles, when we could give them actual human-quality food?

There seems to be a movement afoot to do just that. In America you can buy bone-shaped cookie cutters complete with recipes for homemade granola dog biscuits. And I know a French cat called Dorothy, whose favorite dish is as easy to prepare as opening a can. Bring to a boil half a cup of water, pop in a handful of fresh chicken livers, turn off the stove, let the livers cool in the saucepan, remove, mash with a fork and serve. Now all they have to do is teach Dorothy not to purr with her mouth full. *(Fade up purring.)* For National Public Radio, I'm Alice Furlaud, in Paris.

After sign-out, Dorothy purrs some more, and the "All Things Considered" production mixed this with the triumphal ending of a Brandenburg concerto, which worked beautifully: all Brandenburg concertos would be improved by a little purring in the background.

EATING OUR WAY DOWN TO VENICE

The Dorothy who purrs at the end of that broadcast was the late black-and-white cat of Pati Hill, and a most memorable animal. Pati is an author of some renown: she wrote a lovely book called The Pit and the Century Plant, one of the books I wish I'd written—along with Persuasion, Great Expectations, and The Joy of Cooking. By the time I knew her she had become the founder and doyenne of French photocopy art. But Pati hates flattery from me because she thinks I am incapable of understanding art, whether Rembrandt or the significance of her Xeroxing real things like fish, lettuce leaves and the entire Château of Versailles. (I suspect it has something to do with the juxtaposition of Appearance and Reality, which professors used to go on and on about at Harvard.) I have done two features on Pati, and early in my career she and I went down to Venice on the Orient Express with free tickets, for a reason I will discuss in a later work. The minute we got off the train in Venice, Pati looked around her and said, "I hate this place. I'm going home tonight."

She did, in fact, stay three days, and nearly missed the Orient Express going back to Paris. It stopped for her as she was literally running down the track. Pati is a fount of all wisdom, a sort of Delphic oracle in a never-ironed man's shirt.

Recording the rackety-packety noise of the old Orient Express cars as they bumped along, both from inside and outside, was a challenge for me. But my chef d'oeuvre was the ancient-sounding flush of the train's toilet. I felt it was such an achievement to have held the microphone, flushed the complicated mechanism and kept my balance as the train rocked and creaked along, that when I mixed it with an "All Things Considered" producer, I begged her to let this precious sound go on for ages. But the pacing of radio features isn't based on the *difficulty in getting the sound, and alas, the flushing was given a mere two seconds.*

The piece started with the "all aboard" whistle of the lovely, luxurious pastiche which is the Orient Express today, then from inside the train, rackety-rattly train noise which faded down a little to allow a steward to be heard.

STEWARD: Good evening, madam. Welcome to the Orient Express. Could I have your name please?

ALICE: Um . . . Furlaud.

STEWARD: Yes. You're in cabin 7. Could you just . . .

ALICE: Philosophers talk of the ultimate journey whose destination is unimportant—and this could be it! At $900 for the overnight trip in a single cabin, you don't use the Orient Express as a mere means of transport. To take the Orient Express just to get to Venice would be like taking the $1500 raft trip down the Colorado River just to get from Bullhead City to Yuma. I don't normally travel this way. A friend gave me this trip as a present. But what she didn't give me was the costume to go with it. Most of my fellow passengers were wearing 1920s finery, even though the brochure that came with the ticket, in a shiny wallet with the Orient Express crest on it, only specified black tie at dinner. Two travellers who almost remember the 1920s were gorgeously dressed in jet-beaded flapper clothes from old family trunks.

FIRST FLAPPER: The only problem was the plush chairs. *(Second flapper giggles.)* Her beads and my fringes were getting stuck and we couldn't move!

ALICE: The deep plush chairs in the oriental dining room have flowered patterns on them like carpet bags, and in one of them was an apparent Russian grand duchess. But it turned out her white silk and pearled cloche hat came from Saks Fifth Avenue, this year.

CLOCHE: *(Slight Brooklyn accent)* I just love anything that has to do with that error. I really feel I should have been born then. I love the clothing of it. I love the way people lived at that time. You know, from watching the television *(train lurches)*—and reading about it!

ALICE: Maybe it's the experience of "Masterpiece Theater" these people are after *(cocktail piano music fades up)*, not the experience of the real past. In the bar car, for instance, with its inlaid woodwork and champagne buckets and flowers, I wondered if all those spies and diplomats on the old Orient Express carried on their intrigues to the tune of an actual grand piano. *(More nostalgic piano music, with tinkling of glasses.)* In fact, aside from the engine, which is modern and electric, how much of this train is real anyway? It turns out that the new train was formed of bits and pieces of the old train, with a lot of additions by a French decorator, Gérard Gallet. The end result is apparently a lot more luxurious than in the 1920s. Paul Bianchini, a founding father of this Orient Express, remembers dinner on the old train.

BIANCHINI: *(French accent)* My sister and I and the governess would go to the *wagon restaurant*, and one of my memory is, believe it or not, the dessert. And the dessert was those little chopped fruits that you buy in a can, you know, with a lot of syrup?

ALICE: You mean fruit cocktail, sort of.

BIANCHINI: Fruit cocktail—I mean with the cherry and everything—and this is what to me reminds me of the Orient Express.

ALICE: The dessert I had for dinner was *Gâteau bavarois aux pommes Calvados*—a sort of sculptured tower of cake and cream and liqueur. It was served by waiters probably chosen as much for their romantic mustaches as their sense of balance. The two Cambodian dishwashers I met were chosen, according to some Orient Express PR fellow, because they fit easily into the tiny scullery. But my cabin steward, Duncan, said his job is easy compared to old Orient Express days.

DUNCAN: *(Scottish accent)* I mean you were not more than a serf in those days, I believe. And I think they would be on beck and call twenty-four hours a day. We're quite lucky to get three hours a night, I think.

ALICE: Sylvia Nelson remembers a trip to Constantinople on the Orient Express in 1926.

SYLVIA: *(My mother)* I was with my great aunt, and she took the *Manchester Guardian Weekly*. Wherever we went we had to have that sent ahead—that was the most important thing. And they . . . one of the uses of it was on the train she would laboriously cut out a hole in the middle – of several of them – take one, and go down the hall to the W.C. It embarrassed me beyond everything.

ALICE: And the W.C.'s at the end of each car do take you right back to 1926, with the heavy nickel faucets that snap shut so firmly and the complex pulley and handle that flushes the toilet. In fact, on the Orient Express, it's hard to tell the genuine old thing from the decorator's fantasies. After a few hours I decided I didn't care if the Orient Express was about as authentic as the atomic submarine at Disneyland: I was going to relax and enjoy it. But I did miss one thing you'd expect to find on this famous train: mysterious strangers – the kind travellers used to be warned not to play cards with. I met two men in pith helmets and white gloves who looked promising at first.

FIRST HELMET: Uh, I'm from Syracuse, New York, and we're taking the train to Venice.

ALICE: Are you planning to go on from Venice – further into the bush or some place?

SECOND HELMET: No no no no. The only bush we're going to is in the bar car. We thought we might get lost there, so we wore our pith helmets.

ALICE: The truth is, the magic of the old Orient Express was more the places it went to than the train itself. Mysterious strangers, secret agents and people like that, are usually on their way somewhere important, not indulging in nostalgia travel – and nowadays those types are more likely to be on the People Express than the Orient Express. But this train has one true feature of the 1920s: the lurching, creaking bumpiness of the ride in these old railroad cars. In the middle of the night, in the unair-conditioned panelled library car, swaying and clattering into the Simplon Tunnel through the Alps, there's absolutely nothing between the traveller and the past. *(The squeak of old train brakes and sound of the train entering a station.)* For National Public Radio, I'm Alice Furlaud, arriving in Venice.

(Fade up some grandiose 1930s music suitable for end titles of a Myrna Loy and William Powell romance-and-adventure movie.)

THE GONDOLIERS

If you go in for nostalgia travel, a gondola on a sunny spring day, with the shadows and echoes and music of Venice all around you, beats even the Orient Express. The report I did for "All Things Considered" on my afternoon with the imaginative, patient and generous gondolier Gabriele Focardi, consisted mostly of lots of examples of what Thomas Mann calls "the gondolier's cry, half warning, half salute"—and me talking to myself. I could only record scraps of what Gabriele was telling me from his position behind me, because keeping the microphone anywhere near his mouth, even by kneeling on the cushions, was impossible. I started the piece with a few seconds of Gabriele calling out among the wave sounds, hollow voices and bumps of a small, crowded canal, under the following:

ALICE: A moving gondola is not the place to have an intimate conversation with a gondolier. For one thing, he's standing behind you, high up on the stern of this elegant black boat, facing the bow. And when he's not reciting the history of the palaces and churches along the way, he's likely to be using his single, long oar to do some very tricky navigation—especially tricky when approaching a bridge. (*To Gabriele:*) Was your grandfather a gondolier? Ooh, a complicated maneuver here; we seem to be scraping bottom. We've run aground! Shall I fend off on this side?

GONDOLIER: No, no, no, no!

ALICE: He's bent double, and we've made it through.

GONDOLIER: O! Ohé! Mado premado! (*Or sounds to that effect.*)

ALICE: Traffic jam of gondolas here, going in different directions. The red streamers on their hats, and their striped shirts against the elegant palazzos. . . . (*Gabriele and other gondoliers call to each other, loud and clear.*)

GONDOLIER: My father, my grandfather and all the family are gondoliers. My cousins, my second cousins, my uncles, all are gondoliers. Avanti! Ohé d uno!

ALICE: Gabriele Focardi, the gondolier who's propelling me around Venice in full costume, is called "the Professor" by his colleagues. He has a university degree in oriental studies, and his book about T'ang Dynasty foreign missions to China is being published this year. But at thirty, he is giving up the scholarly life to be a full-time gondolier, partly because of his family tradition and partly because of the money. It costs about $35 an hour to hire a gondola—and gondoliers have a fifty-minute hour. Although gondoliers don't work in the winter, they are thought to earn more than Venetian bank managers.

(*Sound: gondolier tenor voice singing sentimental song fades under following:*)

ALICE: Irino Fagarazzi is fifty-five. He's come back to gondoliering after a long career as an opera singer. He and his gondola—inherited from his father—belong to one of the most elegant gondola stations, as they're called, in Venice: the landing stage of the Gritti Palace hotel, on the Grand Canal. We talked there about the nitty-gritty of the gondolier's life: quarrels between the two rival cooperative societies, differences between the communist and noncommunist gondoliers, and how to qualify. (*Sound: water lapping at the Gritti station.*)

IRINO: When they are sixteen years old they learn how to row the gondola, at eighteen years old they apply to become a substitute, and after a number of years they become a gondolier with a license.

ALICE: And they have to pass a test?

IRINO: Oh, yes, of course, they have to pass a test not just to row the gondola, but they have to be a good person, to be a good swimmer, to save somebody if anything happens, but nothing ever happens! But this is the kind of thing we have to do.

ALICE: And is it a difficult test to pass? I mean is it like the London taxi-driver examination?

IRINO: No, no, but is very difficult, because you have to go in the small canals up and down, back and forward, you cannot touch the wall—you see, it's quite difficult!

ALICE: Yes, if you ram the gondola into the wall, you've had it.

IRINO: You fail the test, anyway, and if you damage the gondola, you have to pay.

(Sound: the loud, lapping, hoot-tooting sound of the Grand Canal.)

ALICE: The Grand Canal, which is Venice's version of Fifth Avenue, only more so, is full of hazards for the gondola: everything, not just tourists, has to be carried around Venice by boat. *(Loud motorboat sound.)* I've never seen a motorboat full of coffins! *(Siren.)* And the ambulance! And the Coca Cola boat, red and white, of course, and full of bottles . . . and there's the garbage boat!

GABRIELLE: Ohé! Limano! Ohé!

ALICE: But to us foreigners, everything about the city of Venice, with its domes and palaces magically rising out of the Adriatic sea, is just pure romance—especially the gondoliers. *(Sound: a group of gondoliers singing on a bridge, with accordion.)*

ALICE: *(To Irino)* Don't girls fall in love with gondoliers all the time?

IRINO: Oh, well, most of the time. A lot of young girls come over here because we have very handsome gondoliers, very young. And a lot of women they fall in love with them, not just for the gondolier, but for the gondola, for Venice, for the moon, people singing—I don't know: it's like a dream in Venice anyway. Because everybody can talk about Venice, but to be in Venice is something different. *(Sound of accordion and singing fades up.)*

ALICE: For National Public Radio, I'm Alice Furlaud, in Venice.

WILD SOUND AT THE AIR SHOW

I hear the philosopher Ivan Ilych, in the kind of book I never can bring myself to actually read, says that any land travel faster than a bicycle or any sea travel faster than a sailing ship is a waste of time. It should naturally follow from this that a gondola is faster than an F-16 jet fighter plane, if you consider the time and energy spent in designing, building and paying for the aircraft. I guess it also follows that the Paris Air Show is the greatest waste of time and motion since the dance marathons of the 1920s. But in a horror-stricken sort of way, this festival fascinates me every time I report on it.

I have met some characters at the Paris Air Shows, my favorite being Joe Thomas, a pilot, animal rights activist and former airport security official. He was fascinated, in 1985, by my pushy questioning of the Air Show security guards, and later sent me a photograph he had taken of me pointing a microphone at a gendarme, to which Joe had added a balloon saying, "And now, mon Capitaine, you can perhaps tell our listeners when the surprise terrorist attack will take place and what your contingency plans are?" Here's my air show feature of that year for "All Things Considered."

HOST: The world's biggest air event, the Paris Air Show, closes on Sunday night, having been visited by an estimated 800,000 people. But the general public was invited in only on the two weekends and one Wednesday for the ten-day show. The rest of the crowd at Le Bourget airport were buyers and sellers of planes for pleasure, business and war. Alice Furlaud did some comparison shopping at the Paris Air Show.

(Sound: the truly wild sound of a fighter plane, tearing through the air, fading under.)

ALICE: (Narrating) It's hard to resist ordering, say, a few F-16 jet fighters at a mere 13 million dollars each, when you're being served a champagne lunch as the plane goes through its death-defying paces in the sky right in front of you. Three hundred fifty aviation companies from various countries have what they call "chalets" – clubhouses – right out on the runway. They've got gardens with fake funeral grass and tables with umbrellas. And jolly military-industrial complex types sit there and make deals and eat *poulet en gelée* while waiters keep refilling their wine glasses. *(Sound: loudspeaker listing characteristics of the Mirage, or Harrier, or whatever the plane is that's ripping through the sky overhead.)* So it was no surprise, the day I had lunch at Airbus Industrie, that Pan Am had just decided to buy twenty-eight French-made Airbusses for a billion dollars. After lunch I spoke to Alan Boyd, Airbus's North American chairman. He used to be the U.S. secretary of transportation.

ALICE: *(At Airbus chalet)* Mr. Boyd, since you've lost your amateur standing, we might say, how much, if I wanted to buy an Airbus, would it cost me – the smallest size?

BOYD: The smallest size you could buy today for 29 million, 600 dollars, and it would be a bargain.

ALICE: It would?

BOYD: Absolutely. It would carry 150 passengers, too, comfortably.

ALICE: Now you get the impression here that it's sort of a country fair, only instead of buying a pig, you're buying a Mirage 2000.

BOYD: I hope nobody's buying a pig! Ha-ha-ha. . . . *(Sound: nearly deafening zooms, alternating with loudspeakers and silences.)*

ALICE: *(Narrating)* Out on the display field there are acres and acres of planes, arranged like toys with their warheads, missiles and bombs laid out neatly in front of them. They give off a strange live energy, as if they might all suddenly take off with a roar. The deadliest *helicopter* I saw was a Sikorsky from Stamford, Connecticut.

SALESMAN: This helicopter that we're marketing is basically for third-world countries.

ALICE: What would they use this for in third-world countries?

SALESMAN: Well – it's got weapons in it, so it'd be used for – war.

91

ALICE: How much is it?

SALESMAN: I don't know.

ALICE: You're missing a sale!

SALESMAN: Wait a minute! Wait a minute! The base price is 2.6 million dollars without weapons. Depending on what systems you buy, you can run it up to a total of about 4½ million U.S. dollars.

ALICE: *(Out on the field)* But the biggest plane in the show—the biggest jumbo jet in the world—is supposedly for peaceful purposes. It's the brand-new Russian Antonov Ruslan, making its first public appearance. It's a grey, snub-nosed hulk, let's see *(reading catalogue)*: 257 feet long with a 215-foot wing span, all decorated with arms and hammers. I'm climbing up into it on a very shaky ladder, being given a hand by a Russian, er, representative . . . Inside it's the most enormous area, and empty. You can see the nails in the . . . it's a very stripped-down-for-work affair with pulleys and exposed pipes and wires. This isn't the kind of plane where the stewardess puts you in your seat with Muzak. There aren't any seats. This Mr. Burilenko who's showing people around is not your usual hard-sell type. He's describing the cargo the Antonov will be taking to Siberia.

BURILENKO: . . . oil eqvipment! Heavy machinery! Excavators! Drills!

ALICE: Can another country order this plane?

BURILENKO: What?

ALICE: I couldn't buy one of these?

BURILENKO: To buy? It seems to me it's very expensive for you.

ALICE: *(Narrating)* From the biggest and ugliest plane in the show, I went to the smallest and prettiest, a crop duster—a dainty dragonfly in the ultralight section.

ALICE: This is the contribution of Weedhopper, from Utah. And it's pink, and on the wings it's got yellow and orange and blue stripes. Excuse me, are you from Weedhopper of Utah?

ERIC: *(Has a German accent)* I'm the licensed manufacturer of Weedhopper of Utah for Europe, Africa, the Middle East and Asia. I've got some gold searchers which are using this in Guyana to go and fetch spare parts for their digging machines.

ALICE: You mean gold prospectors?

ERIC: Exactly.

ALICE: It's utterly divine. How much is it?

ERIC: This? The equivalent of 7,500 dollars.

ALICE: That's the cheapest thing I've ever heard of! (*Narrating, not quite drowned out by noise inside helicopter:*) In the end I chose a yellow-and-white Sikorsky peacetime helicopter as Best in Show, purely because I got a ride home in it. We hovered over the River Seine with the Eiffel Tower gleaming below in the late afternoon light. And I remembered what a French company vice president had said as we watched a sharklike plane diving and spinning above us:

EXECUTIVE: The world is crazy. Fifty million dollars for a killing machine. *Look* at that!

(*Plane: Zoooooom! Rrrrrip!*)

ALICE: For National Public Radio, I'm Alice Furlaud, at Le Bourget Air Field.

THE BIG, FAT PRINCE OF THE AIR

France has a special relationship with aviation, both practical and sentimental. Americans, dazzled by their Wright brothers and Lindbergh, often forget that France also produced aviation pioneers and planes. The French cherish the memory of Blériot, who flew the English Channel in his fragile insect of a plane, the Demoiselle; *and the* Petit Puce, *a tiny plane the size of a fat cow with wings, designed in the 1930s for Everyfrenchman to keep in his backyard. A battered* Petit Puce *is always on display at the Paris Air Show. But the most romantic figure in French aviation history is, of course, Antoine de Saint-Exupéry, hero of the airmail service and author of* The Little Prince. *When Saint-Ex's letters to his adored wife were auctioned off, it was a major and controversial event in the Paris art world. I reported on it for Deutsche Welle's North American program, "Across the Atlantic." Their young American announcer, Betsy Hills, began my feature thus:*

HOST: Antoine de Saint-Exupéry disappeared forty years ago, on July 31, 1944, while flying a Lightning reconnaissance plane somewhere in the embattled French skies. This month there will be a memorial ceremony as well as an important and nostalgic auction of Saint-Exupéry's drawings and letters. Alice Furlaud has been finding more about the man who wrote *The Little Prince.*

ALICE: (*Narrating*) Antoine de Saint-Exupéry was famous for being not only a writer, but an aviator—a pioneer in commercial aviation— a nobleman, a philosopher, a painter, and a lover. But some people who knew him saw him as a childlike person, with the innocence of the wise little prince he wrote about, who lived alone on his own tiny planet and could never understand the strange, adult inhabitants of the other planets. André Henry, now seventy-six, was in Saint-Exupéry's wartime flying squadron.

M. HENRY: Saint-Exupéry a toujours été, si vous voulez, dans l'intimité . . . *(Voice fades down under my translation.)* Saint-Exupéry was always a child with his friends. He was shy; he was *very* shy. *The Little Prince* is written just the way he used to talk when he was telling us anecdotes. Except the little prince doesn't stammer the way Saint-Exupéry did. He acted like a little boy, confiding in you. But he wouldn't say a word in front of more than two or three people. When he didn't want to talk, we'd get him to do card tricks.

ALICE: *(Narrating)* André Henry hadn't heard about the auction, or about the party which opened the pre-auction exhibition. It was in the elegant Paris mansion which is the Aeroclub de France, the aviation club of France. Monsieur Picard, the auctioneer who's going to wield the hammer, showed me around.

PICARD: You see here?

ALICE: That's his driver's license! Duplicata du permis de conduire.

PICARD: Yes, this is a double of his driving license, number 1730, given to him in 1930, yes.

ALICE: Wouldn't you just love to see the car he had? I bet it was a Panhard, or something marvelous. And here's the checkbook on the Fifth Avenue Bank.

PICARD: Yes, on the Feeth Avenue Bank of New York.

ALICE: *(Narrating)* Oh, and I see the little elephant—oh, no! That elephant was one of the sketches for *The Little Prince* that were on display. But most of the exhibits are so personal, it's as if Saint-Exupéry's top bureau drawer had been emptied into the glass cases. A cousin of Antoine de Saint-Exupéry, Jacques de Fontaine, translated Saint-Exupéry's last letter to Consuelo, his obviously adored wife.

FONTAINE: "Mon amour. . . ." My love.

ALICE: And she's kissed it: you can see there's lipstick on the letter.

FONTAINE: "I am very far from you. I cannot tell you where I am. But I am so near you, who lives in my heart. I," er, don't know how to say—

ALICE: "I'm keeping well, I'm keeping well—"

FONTAINE: "I am keeping well, but it can happen to me, *un croc en jambe*," how do you say?

ALICE: Oh, "tripped up": I can be tripped up—

FONTAINE: Yes—"by God, somewhere in France. But you have to know that I don't regret anything, absolutely nothing, even—"

ALICE: "Except to make you cry."

FONTAINE: "Except to make you cry," yes.

ALICE: *(Narrating)* Consuelo de Saint-Exupéry died five years ago and left all these treasures to her chauffeur, who is now selling them. This distresses Saint-Exupéry's relations, including Jacques de la Fontaine.

FONTAINE: He's doing it because all that takes up a lot of room, it is without interest; the only interest is money!

ALICE: *(Narrating)* But André Henry, Saint-Exupéry's old flying companion, remembers the simpler, wartime days when Saint-Exupéry, over flying age at forty-four, flew missions over occupied France in a Lightning plane which he wasn't quite used to.

M. HENRY: Le cockpit, il était vraiment étroit, n'est-ce pas? et Saint-Exupéry était d'une corpulence quand-même assez forte. . . . *(Fades down under translation.)* The cockpit was very small, and Saint-Exupéry was quite plump. So I helped him fit into it. I remember saying "Commander! Watch! Watch out!" We had rear-view mirrors in those planes, just like a car. I said, "You can see who's attacking you!" he said, "Oh, Henry, I won't have time to look behind me; I'll have to keep looking down to be sure I'm flying over the right targets." *(M. Henry fades up speaking French, then is drowned out by the engine of a Lightning plane, which gradually dies down as the plane disappears into the distance.)*

ALICE: *(Narrating)* A few days later, Saint-Exupéry flew off into the blue and never came back. He was a man of action with his head in the clouds; and the last lines of *The Little Prince* seem to describe the way he looked at life. "Look at the sky: ask yourself, has the sheep eaten the flower, or hasn't he? And you'll see how everything changes. And no grown-up person will ever understand how very important that is." I'm Alice Furlaud, in Paris.

THE CLOCHARDS' CLUB

Without statistics or sociological studies to bear me out, it seems to me that in France the treatment of the sick, old and homeless is infinitely better than what I have been seeing in the U.S. The French are not generally thought of as "caring," but you'd never know it if you had visited the convalescent homes and hospitals where friends of mine have been cared for in luxury—free, or nearly free. And private charities here often seem to zero quietly in on real needs, without the hard-sell fuss and fanfare of, say, the Jerry Lewis campaign for the disabled.

For the BBC's "Food Programme" I reported on the Restaurants du Coeur—the distribution of box lunches and shopping bags of groceries personally organized by the late Coluche, France's favorite clown. I did a broadcast on the supermarket chain which gave out free food during 1985, a bad year for the "new poor," and a feature the same year on the Hare Krishna people, who served truly delicious hot meals from the back of a truck in several Paris districts before they were outlawed in France. I had a couple of these dinners standing out in the cold at night near the Pompidou Cultural Center, managing a microphone and a paper cup of lentil soup. For dessert, a basket of polished apples was passed among the hungry drifters by an orange-robed young man with the hospitable politeness of a high-born hostess.

These were all set up for the nouveaux pauvres, the often well-dressed people who were sudden victims of unemployment and inflation. But the poor we have always with us in Paris are the clochards, homeless tramps who live from bottle to bottle, sometimes on the quais by the Seine within the sound of the cloches, or bells, of Notre Dame. These people are the hardest to help, because any pension they get—and there are several different kinds—is immediately spent on drink.

97

Pascale Donckier de Donceel created, twenty years ago, a day-care center for clochards in Belleville, a poor section of Paris better known for its colorful black population and African vegetable stalls than elderly drunks. Pascale, half Belgian, half English, is still only in her early forties. She gave, or raised, the money for this center all herself, buying a vacant lot and building the place from scratch. The City of Paris contributes a small sum toward its upkeep. This is all the recognition she has had from France, but I don't know two worthier candidates for the Legion of Honor than Pascale and her partner, Jean Lottenberg. I started my feature on the Centre Emmanuel with a hubbub of male voices, loudest of all an old, drunkenly warbled French song—sounds that might have been heard in the down-and-out world of Paris since the days of François Villon.

CLOCHARD: De mon enfance, a la la! *(Revelrous shouts.)*

ALICE: Pascale, I'd like—she's waving goodbye to someone—I'd like to ask you how this all started. This is your operation, this has nothing to do with the state, city, or anything, has it?

PASCALE: Well, I had the idea quite a long time ago, because there were a few soup kitchens in Paris but there was no day center. I was quite young at that period, and I thought it was very anonymous—that distribution of soup. And the people used to just take their soup and go away: who was the person who just ate his soup and went away? So I thought it was absolutely necessary to have a day center to get to know these people.

(She's drowned out by the song, ending in a wildly hoarse laugh—a contrast to Pascale's pure, almost nunlike voice.)

ALICE: The room is so simple it might have looked bleak, except that these fifty or so clochards—mostly middle-aged men—give it the atmosphere of a club, not a shelter. Pascale is serving coffee and gâteaux; the people just came down from the Alcool Anonyme meeting upstairs, and the jostling and joking don't interfere with the board games going on at the tables. One Scrabble player has formed a sadly appropriate word: *boire*—to drink.

PASCALE: It happens to be that word, but it's quite a—an accident. *(Leads the way to the kitchen.)* They're all alcoholics, or they are mentally disturbed, and they all live in the road. They have what they call *planques*, they live anywhere which they call a planque. It can mean sleeping in a car, or in corridors, or in caves, or in the Metro. It's a terrible life being a clochard.

ALICE: *(Narrating)* Pascale Donckier de Donceel lived briefly on the Paris streets herself.

PASCALE: I think they're wonderful, really, because I couldn't live there myself three days! Once I tried to live three days that way and I got terribly thin. But I didn't really do it properly because I slept in a church and places like that. So you know, I didn't dare sleep really in the road. Anyway, it's not for me, you know. Oh! Terrible!

ALICE: But you have tried it. Wasn't it terribly cold?

PASCALE: Was it cold! It was just absolutely impossible! Oh, no, these people are extraordinary. They have some kind of strength in them to be able to support that kind of life, you know.

ALICE: *(Narrating)* Pascale's partner in running the center, Jean Lottenberg, has been even closer to the street scene than she has.

JEAN: I lived on the street myself. I was in the street myself. *(His voice—middle-aged, quiet, experienced and a little husky—has a resonance as if speaking in a church or a cloister.)*

ALICE: How long?

JEAN: Not very long.

ALICE: A week?

JEAN: Oh, no, more than a week! One year. For myself, it was quite pleasant.

ALICE: It was!

JEAN: *(A slight chuckle)* Yes, it was.

ALICE: Even in winter?

JEAN: Even in the winter. At that time it was quite pleasant.

ALICE: What were you doing before all this happened?

JEAN: I was working. I was working in ladies' dresses.

ALICE: What?

JEAN: Ladies' dresses.

ALICE: Jean is swabbing off a wound of one of these people here. He's got one eye, and he's got a terrible gash right from his knee to his ankle. He's got a very red face; and Jean is swabbing the wound off with Dakin, a sort of disinfectant.

ALICE: *(Narrating)* I asked Jean Lottenberg whether it was a good idea to give handouts to beggars on the Paris streets.

JEAN: We think that it doesn't help to give a piece of money to someone who's drunken. The piece of money will not help him, it will just help him to buy another bottle of wine.

ALICE: It must be very difficult, I should think, to know where to stop. I mean, don't people come to you with problems and you find yourselves becoming total social workers?

PASCALE: No. We're very lucky to have begun by not entering into that kind of contact, do you see what I mean? When they come here they don't ask for anything: they just suddenly realize they're in a place where they can just sit. And they're not asked for anything, and so they don't ask for anything. They're just themselves. And that's all we want. *(More inebriated song and laughing: "Mamman est une grande Etoile, la la la la la, ha ha. . . . .")*

The most interesting thing I learned from Pascale and Jean came out weeks after I'd finished my report on their friends among the "old poor." Jean told me that lots of clochards carry a tie and a cleanish shirt in their coat pockets in order to crash the many receptions that are given in Paris at the drop of a hat. Some clochards live for days on the champagne and dainty canapés served at these events. Now that I know this, I don't complain much about the customary greediness of the French at Ministry of Culture buffets, or vernissages in the richer art galleries. Who knows, this may be somebody's first meal in two days.

PIGEONS AT MY WINDOW
AND ELSEWHERE

I used to think that if I ever got started Really Writing (I was still thinking this at age fifty), I would like to write like one of these wondrous women who go and look at mud flats or disused quarries, and in whom the tiniest bit of skunk cabbage will trigger tremulously profound thoughts, the resulting books ending up beside the beds of everybody I know. These women are so incredibly sensitive, with such a leisurely thoughtfulness, that I feel they must have rich husbands or fathers. Not having their depth of vision, I hate them, which is not fair, because out of sheer envy and loathing I rarely read past their first chapters. The one I envy most, Anne Morrow Lindbergh, did have a very rich husband – and father, too, I think – but I can forgive her anything, not just because of her suffering or her courage as an aviator, but because of her lovely title, *Listen! the Wind.**

But all of those ladies, dead or alive, are safely inside: inside just what, I'm not sure, but I know they're not out here flapping away on the line like me. They're bound to be inside the right literary circles, the right protest movements – certainly inside the perfectly right country houses, with the right studies to write in – quiet sanctuaries with long French windows, so they can look up from their manuscripts lying on their nice old Sheraton desks and see – what? – the first gleam of snowdrops against the sodden brown grass or something, which sets off another stream of pellucidly phrased thoughts. Oh, how I detest them.

---

* Wait a minute! Is this an original title, or could it, perish the thought, have come (via *Bartlett's Familiar Quotations*) from a poem by Humbert Wolfe (1885-1940) called "Autumn (Resignation)": "Listen! the wind is rising / And the air is wild with leaves / We have had our summer evenings, / Now for October eves"?

I have long French windows, too—literally French windows. One looks out on the courtyard of a seventeenth-century palace, while from the other I can just barely see the central spire of Notre Dame at the end of a long, straight street which, if you don't count the river, leads right to the north transept. I was inspired to write about pigeons by a book called something like *Free-lance Writing for a Living*. Its example of the very worst subject you could possibly write about was "The Pigeons at My Window."

My front window has a balcony about a foot wide. Every morning I used to scatter bread crumbs and bird seed on it. The minute I opened the window, a squadron of pigeons would zoom straight at me down this street, apparently right from Notre Dame itself. For several years, a black pigeon was almost always first. Somehow over the years, the flock narrowed down to a faithful couple of pigeons, Walter and Greer. We knew they were always the same two, because Greer had a lame leg with a big lump around knee level. They made a sort of surrealist semblance of a nest—a paper clip, a fragment of a basket from the market downstairs and things, but they rarely used any of the strands of wool I put out for them. One day we got a glimpse of a white egg in the vague vicinity of this nest. For weeks Greer spent most of her time sitting on it. Walter flapped awkwardly around, even after the hatching of a hideous, spiky, yellowish chick, but he left his family at night. We watched Greer rushing at the chick, pushing it around, teaching it to fly. We watched them in the winter, ruffled up and shivering on the freezing stone. I wanted to bring them all in and give them a bath and keep them forever. But in the summer, we sublet the apartment to an American couple who, in spite of a firm agreement to feed Walter and Greer every day, cut off the food supply the minute our backs were turned and chased them away.

Now I feed pigeons outdoors. I used to do this every spring several times a week in the company of a friendly group of old down-and-outs, hard-core pigeon feeders, who sat every day in a little park by the Seine. This pigeon club seems to have broken up, although I occasionally meet one of its members on the street. In their heyday they used to be greatly amused at my efforts to record their flock of pigeons in the act of taking off en masse. I wasted miles of tape waiting for these moments. When they'd suddenly go up and away, half the time the flap-flapping would be too loud for the level I had set on my tape recorder.

For all I know, some of those pigeons may have recognized me from the old balcony days.

PLANNED PARENTHOOD
FOR PIGEONS

HOST: (*Noah Adams, in fact, of "All Things Considered"*) The concept of Paris in the spring has been a distant myth this year, but sunny days are getting more and more frequent, and Alice Furlaud has been renewing her acquaintance with some natives of Paris—the pigeons and the Parisians who feed them.

(*Sound of roo-cooing pigeons fades under.*)

ALICE: (*Speaking from the riverside*) My usual pigeon-feeding place is a little gravelly strip of park by the Seine. Pigeons sit in a row on the iron railings overlooking the river, hoping for a handout of French bread, which is the favorite food of Paris pigeons. The regular pigeon feeders are just now beginning to appear on the few green benches under the weeping willows, and the most faithful of these is Madame Camille. Every spring for five years or so, I've often found her dozing on a bench with a pigeon perched on her hat and others rummaging in her many shopping bags.

MADAME CAMILLE: I like them a lot. But they are a little bit—how shall I say—they stay too long! (*Tremendous roo-cooing and rustling is heard.*)

ALICE: There are five on your lap right this minute, eating out of your hand, eating right out of the bag.

MADAME CAMILLE: They are tiresome sometimes! (*She laughs—a real laugh, from the heart.*)

ALICE: But she stays very still to let the pigeons roost on her, and I've never seen her shake them off. Most of them are the usual pale grey with black bars on their tails and iridescent green-and-purple neck feathers. But there are charcoal-grey pigeons and black ones, and an occasional brown-and-white pigeon. (*Sound of Madame Camille speaking French and laughing with other pigeon feeders.*) Madame Camille's brown coat and her cracked, laced-up boots and her face and hands have an apparently permanent patina of dirt. Her round hat appears to date from the 1930s, and she herself has seen better days. She remembers an American she knew in Paris when she was in the dress business sixty years ago.

MADAME CAMILLE: A delightful lady! She used to buy dresses and blouses for her shop here. She was delightful! Miss Cronin. But she must be dead since thirty years. Ha, ha! She used to be fifty in 1925! (*A gale of laughter!*)

ALICE: Madame Camille's joie de vivre hasn't been diminished by living mostly out of doors in harsh climate. She says the water she gets from the spigot at the flower market across the river is the purest in the world. And she loves the territory she shares with the pigeons along the river Seine.

MADAME CAMILLE: I like very much the Ile St. Louis because it is very artistic and romantic.

ALICE: Don't you love the church of St. Gervais which is right over there, I can just see it.

MADAME CAMILLE: Have they got services with music?

ALICE: Yes, at 5:30 every day.

MADAME CAMILLE: But they've got a nice service at Notre Dame, too.

(*Sound of bells of Notre Dame, over following narration:*)

ALICE: The pigeons who live among the towers and sculptures of Notre Dame are the descendants of those who moved in when the cathedral was first built in the twelfth century. And their ancestors were wild rock doves who lived in the chalky cliffs along the Seine. The city government of Paris officially recognizes that pigeons are Parisians, too. After all, pigeons saved the day in the Franco-Prussian War by carrying messages into and out of Paris during the siege. But the city wants to cut down its pigeon population from the present estimated 40,000 to about 25,000: so twice a year they distribute grains for the pigeons, treated with birth-control medicine.

Ordinary citizens can be fined 300 to 600 francs—up to $85—for feeding pigeons. Lucky for Madame Camille this law is rarely enforced.

Life can be hard for street pigeons here. In the yellow pages, pest control companies offer to "depigeonize" your courtyard: *dépigeonisation* they call it. Pigeons freeze to death, or get eaten by cats or run over by busses. But to many Parisians, including the homeless who share their hardships, a flock of pigeons taking off into the Paris sky gives a great lift to the spirit. And on the ground, pigeons are an endless source of interest.

MADAME CAMILLE: Oh, look! They are kissing! *(Sounds of roo-cooing, or roucoulements, as the French say.)*

ALICE: The pigeons are kissing?

MADAME CAMILLE: It's very amusing! Ha, ha, ha, ha-ha!

(Sound of cooing, then a great flapping and fluttering of huge flock of pigeons taking off up into the air and under the sign-out.)

ALICE: For National Public Radio, I'm Alice Furlaud, in Paris.

MAI SOIXANTE-HUITE

I was not in Paris in May 1968: my husband and I had been lent a little cottage near Toulon. The South of France had its own version of "the events": no gasoline, few groceries, one-half hour of television a night, which we watched in a tiny bar in Toulon and which consisted entirely of various government officials saying reassuring things. Occasionally a procession of workers would thread through the streets carrying black flags and singing, for some reason, "Frère Jacques." The words were probably different than the song I had learned as a child, but it, too, was reassuring. What I wouldn't give to have been at the Sorbonne!

The month-long student revolt of May '68, which widened into a paralyzing general strike, has never left the forefront of French consciousness. Bloodier things happened in that year of international ferment: the Soviet invasion of Czechoslovakia, the murders of Martin Luther King and Robert Kennedy. But for the French, 1968 means only the trauma and euphoria of those thirty days which shook France. For "All Things Considered," I talked to some participants in that cultural revolution to mark its twentieth anniversary. My report started with sounds of tear-gas bombs exploding, students shouting and shrieking, police sirens and the hee-haw of ambulances—the actual sounds of the "night of the Rue Gay Lussac."

ALICE: *(Narrating over this battle sound)* The revolution erupted unexpectedly. A battle between right-wing and left-wing students led to a police invasion of the sacred precincts of the Sorbonne on May 2nd. The police came out of the university with several vanloads of student prisoners, and that was *ras le bol*, or the last straw, for the hitherto docile students. All month, day and night, thousands of them demonstrated in the Latin Quarter, countered by policemen wielding clubs and hurling tear gas with a violence unknown before in France. Hundreds on both sides were often wounded in a single clash. It looked to many people just like the first stage of another full-fledged French Revolution. Not to former president Valéry Giscard d'Estaing, whose life-style has often been compared to that of Louis XIV.

GISCARD: No, it was not a political revolution like 1789. It was not a social revolution like the Commune in 1870, in which the working class revolted against the bourgeoisie; it was a cultural uprising, and probably the first in French history.

COHN-BENDIT: It wasn't a political revolution at the end because we didn't change the political structure of the country. I always say, politically we lost, socially we win.

ALICE: (*Narrating*) That's Daniel Cohn-Bendit, the guiding spirit of the whole rebellion. He emerged as top student leader during the night-long battle of May 10th on the Rue Gay Lussac, which set a new and savage pace for the revolt.

(*Sound: Gay Lussac battle sounds beginning, "C'est nous les barricades!" — it's we who are the barricades! — and continuing with explosions, shouts, etc., fade under:*)

ALICE: (*Narrating*) Students spontaneously set up barricades of burning cars, overflowing garbage cans, even trees they'd cut down — and cobblestones. The cobblestones could also be heaved out of windows onto the heads of the riot police. (*More sound of riot, then French woman's voice begins:*)

FRENCH WOMAN: Et dans la nuit, les étudiants, etc. (*Fades down under voice-over.*) These students arrived at my parents' apartment on the Rue Gay Lussac with a lot of cobblestones, and they installed themselves in the windows for the whole night. And, you know, a young man with a cobblestone can be very dangerous! My parents weren't favorable to the ideas of the students, but they fed them. And in the morning my father found his car on a barricade with the roof completely smashed in! (*She laughs with great delight.*)

SARAH: I remember people trying to climb up the garden fences and so on, total panic. And then you saw people being hit and dragged away. And, uh, the Sorbonne was transformed in a sort of hospital.

All over the corridors and so on there were people that had been injured and that were being taken care of. I mean, we were all very naive, but we thought, "This is it," you know? "We're leading the revolution and we're changing the world and everybody is scared of us!" And that was the great, I find the great moment.

MICHEL: There was an atmosphere of feast, of festivity, like perhaps in Berkeley, I think in California they had the same thing going on.

ALICE: *(Narrating)* But unlike Berkeley, there was no counterculture already separating the young from the old. Most of the French student warriors of '68 had short hair and old-fashioned manners. It must have been a shock to many French people to hear sociology student Daniel Cohn-Bendit interviewed on the radio just like a real grown-up:

COHN-BENDIT: *(On radio in 1968)* Danny Cohn-Bendit, étudiant en sociologie à la faculté de Nanterre. La répression était voulue, elle a été provoquée . . . *(Fades down.)*

ALICE: *(Narrating)* Danny was hoarse with exhaustion after a night on the barricades of the Rue Gay Lussac, as he explains now, twenty years later:

COHN-BENDIT: This was the 10th of May after this night. Well, we didn't sleep very much in this time, and that's the voice of someone who is very deep in a movement and more acting than sleeping.

COHN-BENDIT: *(On radio)* C'est une répression voulue organisé?

ALICE: *(Narrating)* Danny the Red, as he was called then, is forty-two now. He's a newspaper editor in Frankfurt, Germany, and he looks like a cross between Boris Becker and Raggedy Andy. Why did all those students turn to him as leader in '68?

COHN-BENDIT: I had the capability to say the right thing at the right moment. I was the loudspeaker. I was the one who could give words to the emotions of people in a certain moment, and this made me one of the leaders of the movement.

ALICE: What was the most exciting or frightening moment that you remember?

COHN-BENDIT: Well, the most exciting thing was the 9th of May, the barricades, when you have thirty or forty thousand people building barricades. I mean, this was the beginning of a new spirit, you know? People on the street beginning to talk each to the other, and this, I think, was the great moment.

ALICE: *(Narrating)* A great moment for Monsieur Giscard d'Estaing, then head of a middle-of-the-road political party, was when he realized this wasn't going to be a very dangerous revolution. He picked up a student demonstrator hitchhiking out of the Latin Quarter.

GISCARD: And I said to her, "do you want society to be entirely changed?" "Yes, entirely. We must revamp the French society, and we must destroy all the traditional values and create a new world which will be happier, healthier, and so we must go till the end, to revolution." I said to her, "But why are you hitchhiking from here? You don't stay in the Quartier Latin for the whole revolution?" And she said to me, "No, no no, I want to come back to sleep every night in my parents' home." Ha, ha, ha! So it was—ha, ha—a balanced revolution. *(Monsieur Giscard D'Estaing's laugh here sounds rather like the wolf's upon the entrance of Little Red Riding Hood.)*

ALICE: *(Narrating)* Sarah Lambert was one of the revolutionaries who went home to her parents every night. She was a high-school student of sixteen, but she skipped school and helped out every day during the month-long student occupation of the Sorbonne—an institution which till then had been grimly impersonal.

SARAH: I took part in several discussions there and actually spoke at the Sorbonne in front of the crowd, talking about police violence.
(Sound: girl student speaks emotionally at Sorbonne about police brutality.) There were crowds of people walking in to see what was happening and find out what the students intended to do. Things were happening all the time, and you were organizing meetings to discuss all sorts of different things.

ALICE: *(Narrating)* But the well-known wine journalist, Michel Smith, was a twenty-year-old reporter for *Paris Match* in 1968. He remembers the women in the Sorbonne occupation as not very politically involved.

MICHEL: But they were much freer, I mean they took their bra off, and their pants off, and that's it!

COHN-BENDIT: At that time we were revolting against all the social structure and the social morals. And we were revolting against the Vietnam War, we were revolting against the way the university was organized, what we were teached. We were revolting at the end for another way of life.

ALICE: *(Narrating)* Meanwhile, back at the presidential palace, the defenders of the old way of life were getting nervous. Workers were following the students' example and closing down factories and shipyards and post offices all over the country. The Communist unions joined in only at the last minute.

COHN-BENDIT: Well, but this wasn't done by the Communists. This was done by young workers, it was done by little workers' groups who, because of the movement, felt that it was possible to change more. And the Communists were obliged to follow.

ALICE: *(Narrating)* And the students occupied theaters and opened them to the public for free discussions. France's only television station—government-controlled—was closed by the strike. Transport ground to a halt, gasoline was unobtainable, grocery stores were ransacked for staple foods. President de Gaulle, France's towering military hero since World War II, kept ducking out of sight for days at a time. Prime Minister Pompidou was left to try and reassure the public on the single half hour of television that was allowed per day.

Finally, President de Gaulle made a secret helicopter trip to Germany, it's thought to rally the support of French army officials, just in case. And on May 30th, he returned, just like Papa who comes home and finds the naughty children not in bed yet, and gave everybody a sound scolding on TV.

(Sound: General de Gaulle's speech, beginning, "Françaises! Français!" fades down under following:)

ALICE: *(Narrating)* The very same day, hundreds of thousands of people from all over France marched up the Champs Elysées to the Arc de Triomphe to support the general. They sang the "Marseillaise" around the tomb of the Unknown Soldier, where, three weeks before, the students had sung the "Internationale." The Revolution That Might Have Been, for all intents and purposes, was over.

(Sound: General de Gaulle, "Le peuple Français tout entier!")

110

ALICE: *(Narrating)* Some direct results of '68 happened six years later, when Monsieur Giscard d'Estaing became president of France: abortion was legalized and eighteen-year-olds got the vote. But French people give May '68 the credit, or the blame, for all sorts of changes: the closing of the generation gap, the end of filling out police forms at hotel registry desks, the increased use of the familiar *tu* instead of *vous*, blue jeans, women's liberation, the rise of the electric guitar, the decline of the five-course meal.

COHN-BENDIT: Well, '68 is the beginning of all that!

ALICE: . . . says Daniel Cohn-Bendit.

COHN-BENDIT: Sixty-eight is the beginning of thousands of possibilities. And the realization of possibilities is after — in the '70s, '80s, '90s, the year 2000, I think.

ALICE: *(Narrating)* But whatever possibilities have or haven't yet been fulfilled, those heady days of May in Paris twenty years ago — their innocence and euphoria and openness, could never have lasted. Michel Smith and Sarah Lambert remember:

MICHEL: You could say anything you wanted in those days. Even you could say the food was disgusting and nobody would dare to throw you out. It was a period where one could say *anything,* and I don't know of anybody who didn't use this period to say everything they had on their minds.

SARAH: *(Her voice trembling as if near tears)* It was just this incredible — like a party! But that lasted for days, and days, and days — you know? *(Sound: students singing in a large chorus, over sounds of rioting, sirens, explosions, fades up under sign-out.)*

ALICE: For National Public Radio, I'm Alice Furlaud, in Paris.

Big Sur And The Camelot
Of The Psyche

Behind the students who threw paving stones at the French police-
men, and indeed behind the ghastly murders by the Charles Manson
cult in California, there was a tidal wave of consciousness transfor-
mation which ebbed away without being reported in the news, except
in a few, usually sarcastic, asides. It's in the nature of the media to
be attracted to political events, no matter how insignificant most of
them are in the long run; and to crime—no matter how stupid an
expression it may be of everyone's yearnings. There wasn't any way
the newspapers could chronicle the fact that inner individual changes
more powerful than the political kind were happening all the time
during "the events" of 1968.

In that year I was dragged kicking and screaming onto the Path
to Enlightenment, or more specifically, out to the Esalen Institute,
that community high on a cliff above the Pacific in Big Sur, Califor-
nia, where the American "human potential movement" began amidst
the screams of people being reborn or rolfed. Max and I lived in or
around Esalen for the next three years, and on Esalen's 25th anniver-
sary I wrote this memoir for "All Things Considered." I recorded it
several times but couldn't keep my voice from trembling at the mem-
ory of Esalen's high hippie heyday, as Sarah Lambert's did when she
remembered the French student riots. I started the commentary with
a quote from A Tale of Two Cities which has been done to death this
year, the 200th anniversary of the French Revolution. But it didn't
sound hackneyed in 1987.

SCRIPT: "It was the best of times, it was the worst of times," as
Charles Dickens said of the French Revolution—and what we
experienced at Esalen in 1968 was a true revolution of consciousness.

112

As we lay out in the hot sulphur baths with the Pacific waves pounding in our ears, or shouted and wept in the group rooms, we really believed that this revolution would spread everywhere and transform the world.

We were a wildly varied group: the professional therapists, or group leaders; the paying customers who came for the five-day groups and discovered more joy; the gypsy hippie staff and their hangers-on who lived around the edges in trees, under bridges and waterfalls, wherever they could cling, just to be part of this place where all the energy and the hope of the universe seemed to be focused. And there were the Resident Fellows: I was one of these selected interns, or you might call them officer candidates—a dozen or so of us, give or take a few casualties, got a powerful four-month cocktail of rolfing, encounter, gestalt therapy, sensory awareness, Alexander method, Feldenkreis, acupuncture, bioenergetics, T'ai Chi, the Synanon game and the unique and lovely Esalen message. We also worked, in this boot camp of the psyche. We cleaned the guest cabins and weeded and washed dishes and got up at 5:30 to cook breakfast. And when our four months were over, we took all sorts of wonky Big Sur jobs just to cling on to those cliffs and stay a part of Esalen.

All of this fluctuating community was turned on, not by drugs—although LSD was dropping like gentle acid rain from heaven—but simply by honesty and awareness. We acquired these painfully in psychologist William Schutz's encounter groups that set the pace at Esalen in those days. We smashed our fists into pillows called Mother, and we took off all our clothes and floated on floods and floods of tears into strange states of consciousness—and saw each other and ourselves as we really were. And although honesty about one's feelings may seem an oversimplified solution to the world's problems, we were *positive* that among things sure to die out when it caught on were head trips, greed, drugs in mental institutions, psychoanalysis and, just possibly, war.

We all moved around this magic collection of cabins between the mountains and the sea, in a state of being known as the Esalen High. You didn't feel happy or sad or wise, but you were just slowed down, like walking through molasses. Things like putting a dime in the pay telephone could be quite difficult. And in the outside world you had sex appeal for all and sundry.

The theme music to it all was Lay lady lay across mah big brass bed, and she touched your perfect body with her mind. I remember

Joan Baez singing to us on the lawn—not a record, but the real Joan. I remember the smell of eucalyptus trees and huge black-and-orange butterflies, and I remember cutting my hand on the carrot-shredding machine and having it stitched up on the floor by a naked doctor with a naked nurse in attendance. I remember we were often bullied by the management: it's easy to bully people whose souls are newly open to the skies. I remember Esalen's 8th birthday party, of which for some reason I was in charge. The group leaders, the giants that stalked the earth in those days, were the waiters. They cheerfully rushed around with loaded trays—even Will Schutz, even Mike Murphy, owner and creator of Esalen. He benevolently let it take different directions from the quiet, spiritual atmosphere it began with. Now I hear it has an intellectual approach, still nourishing and inspiring people—but the crazy, risky, high, high Esalen where we were aware of the very atoms bubbling around in our bodies and lived in that fourth-dimensional state of truth which we were sure would turn on all mankind—is gone. I use the word *mankind* advisedly. Those were the pre-women's lib days when Esalen girls shimmered around in long skirts and whispered, "I'm into baking bread." Maybe they were somewhat silly. But when I see the girls of today clicking along Madison Avenue in their knife-sharp gabardine suits carrying their portable computers, I ache for what they'll never know, and what they'll never be.

So what did you get out of it, people say to me. You look the same as any other worried lady at the checkout counter. I don't know. What *do* you get out of having discovered that what we think of as reality is but a dream? Nothing much. It's discombobulating and it doesn't lead to success or stability. But if you'd done it, you wouldn't have missed it for the world.

La Chasse Aux Champignons

Microphones and mycologists do not mix. The mushroom hunters I tried to follow around the forest of St. Cloud acted as paranoid as if they were beating the bushes for billion-franc caches of cocaine or diamonds—not merely wild mushrooms which they were going to make into soup, or just possibly add to a collection. Reporting on the best mushroom autumn season for years for the BBC's "Food Programme," I had to run after the fleet-footed members of the Mycological Club of France, aiming my microphone at them as they waved me off, crashing through the underbrush like frightened deer. There's a lot of panting in the actualities for this piece.

When I learned that this club was spending a Sunday out mushrooming in the woods, I had pictured a friendly stroll, picking a bolet here and there, with a nice long pause for lunch. In fact there was not a pause until the mid-afternoon train back, and I don't remember a single moment of conviviality the whole day. These mushroom fanatics are so competitive they don't even hunt in pairs; and yet all sixty of them had gathered at the Gare Saint-Lazare around their leaders and set off together like good little children.

This is one of the great French paradoxes: they do everything in large groups, from formulating philosophies to going to the beach, and yet the concept of cooperation is practically unknown in France. The enormous French bourgeois families—who flourish right now, not just in Jean Renoir movies—stick close together and make few friends outside the family; but within the family they tear each other to furious shreds.

I started off my 1985 report with the wild blare of the leader's hunting horn: it sounded more suitable for an eighteenth-century wild boar hunt than a mushroom expedition.

(Ambience: blasts of the horn, anxious chattering, more horn sound under the following narration:)

ALICE: These were hard-core French mushroom freaks, and even though they were all armed with baskets, picnics with French bread and wine were not on their agendas. The members of the Club Mycologique de France arrived at the St. Cloud station together under the supervision of two leaders, who wore microscopes around their necks and carried large Siegfried-like hunting horns. But once in the woods, the club members scattered like children on an Easter-egg hunt. Occasionally someone would bring a mushroom to the leaders to be identified. But basically it was each man for himself in the mad dash for mushrooms. They peered around rocks and stumps and under bushes, looking for *girolles*, *bolets*, *mousserons*, *chanterelles*, *gyromites* and other mushrooms – some to eat, others to peer at, smell and take home to dissect. Unlike most French people, these amateur mycologists were much too intent on their finds to chat. Madame Besançon is a doctor.

ALICE: *(In the forest)* Madame Besançon has found one. What do you think it is?

MADAME BESANCON: I don't know, I don't know. Maybe a *russole*.

ALICE: It's very deadly looking! A slightly greeny purple.

MADAME BESANCON: Green *russole*, I think.

ALICE: Oh! here's a lovely one. Salmon-colored. A sort of underwater look.

MADAME BESANCON: *Paxille. Paxille enroulé.*

ALICE: Aha, I'll bet this is a deadly *amanita*.

MADAME BESANCON: We must ask.

ALICE: I saw a man over there eating one already. Isn't he a little bit daring?

MADAME BESANCON: Completely fanatic.

ALICE: *(Narrating)* The fanatic was an elderly retired pilot, whose basket was brimming with curly yellow and pink mushrooms. He paused for just a few expert words before rushing off into a thicket. *(Note: he didn't precisely pause, but was cornered by me against a tree.)*

ALICE: Now that's really poisonous-looking, it's got purple gills. What do you think that is?

EX-PILOT: This one? It's called a *pied bleu.*

ALICE: A blue foot?

EX-PILOT: A blue foot, yes.

ALICE: Do you think it's edible?

EX-PILOT: (*Impatiently*) Yes.

ALICE: There's something about blue mushrooms which doesn't look edible, if you know what I mean.

EX-PILOT: Aaaaaaargh! (*Exasperated by my questions, he rushes off.*)

MADAME BESANCON: C'est un champignon que je vois là-bas? (*Crashing sound as she in turn escapes from me into the bushes.*)

(*Sound: the piercing bray of a French ambulance is heard on outskirts of the forest.*)

ALICE: (*Narrating*) That ambulance in the distance reminded me that about twenty of these enthusiasts die every year in France, poisoned by wild mushrooms they've gathered themselves. Michelle Hurault is the librarian of the cryptogamy section of the Museum of Natural History:

MME. HURAULT: My grandmother told me when she was young, she comes from the South of France, and lots of people had very few to eat . . .

ALICE: Very little to eat?

MME. HURAULT: Very little to eat. So they used to go to the forest to pick mushrooms. And one day a whole family went in the forest, and they eat mushrooms that they have gathered in the forest and the day after, they all died. That was awful! And this happens once in a while, even now.

(*Sound: eager gabble of large crowd of children in the museum.*)

ALICE: (*Narrating*) This is why all twelve-year-olds in the French school system are taught how to tell one wild mushroom from another. There was a big crowd of children at an exhibit of about 400 varieties of mushrooms—lots of them gathered by Michelle

Hurault herself—at the Museum of Natural History in the Jardin des Plantes—which also houses a zoo. I asked a few of them if they were cramming a lot of mushroom knowledge into their notebooks.

BOY: Yes!

ALICE: Which mushroom do you like the best?

BOY: Amanita printanière.

ALICE: Why do you like that best?

BOY: It's a nice one, and, um . . .

ALICE: But couldn't it kill you?

BOY: Yes!

ALICE: Is that why you like it?

BOY: Yes!

(*Sound: busy market, with cries of vendors, barrows, etc.*)

ALICE: (*Narrating*) But while that deadly *amanita printanière* is an innocent-looking pinko-grey, the black, flowerlike mushroom called "the trumpet of death" is edible—in fact delicious. I bought some in the market, the Marché Maubert near Notre Dame, and I cooked them with two of the five or so other kinds of wild mushrooms they had for sale. Wild mushrooms have an earthy, perfumy flavor: not at all like the cultivated white buttons you get in supermarkets. But mushrooms on toast for one cost me sixty-seven francs—almost seven pounds. It was consoling to think that at least they were cheaper than truffles.

It's not only their ability to nourish or poison us which fascinates people about mushrooms. It's also their origin. Mushrooms are cryptogams: plants which don't need photosynthesis to develop. Professor Jeanne Cobbi is an ethnobiologist who studies eating habits around the world. In her laboratory in a hidden corner of the Sorbonne, we talked about the mysteriousness of mushrooms.

ALICE: You don't feel that they have long roots, that they have seasons.

JEANNE: They have seasons, they don't have roots, but they have seasons. And they have rhythm. And they have deep contact with the weather and the atmosphere. You know they are children of the humidity, they are produced by earth and humidity, and how you say—obscurity.

ALICE: Darkness?

JEANNE: Darkness! Thank you.

ALICE: *(Narrating)* It may be this idea of darkness that intrigues us in mushrooms. Perhaps they put us in touch with primeval forces, with the earth as it was before God said, "Let there be light!" This may add to some people's fear of mushrooms. Jeanne Cobbi:

JEANNE: English-speaking people don't like mushrooms, especially wild mushrooms. When the Queen Elizabeth came to France as guest of the French government, one of the meals which they prepared in the Palais de l'Elysée where the Président de la République gave the lunch, they planned on the menu wild mushrooms served with meat. They were to be girolles which we consider the best mushrooms we have, which are beautiful to see, which are very nice, with a good smell, and which are completely secure—safe. You can't confuse them with another kind of mushroom. But the Ambassador of Great Britain in Paris decided it was not a good idea and demanded the French government take this mushroom out of the menu, and to give her something else. *(She giggles.)* I think it was just because it was wild mushrooms, and the idea of giving wild mushrooms to the Queen Elizabeth was a big risk.

(Sound: the murmur of visitors on the opening day of the French Post Office's mushroom exhibit. This heard under the following narration:)

ALICE: A risk of what? Were they afraid the Queen would be poisoned, or go on a magic mushroom trip? At another mushroom exhibition, this time at the Ministry of the Post Office, with over 500 varieties all gathered by postmen, there was a big poster with colors for the different categories of mushroom. A red dot for mortel, or deadly poison; pink for toxic, green for indigestible, yellow for harmless and blue for edible. There wasn't any category for hallucinogenic, and yet mind-changing mushrooms are having their own record crop this fall. In fact, they've just been discovered by drug traffickers. On display at the Post Office Ministry was the amanita tue-mouche, or fly killer, listed merely as "toxic." It's red with white dots, right out of Snow White and the Seven Dwarfs, and it

119

supposedly causes hallucinations of Disneyland proportions. But the Post Office officials in charge just didn't want to know.

OFFICIAL: Non! Non-non-non-non-non-non!

ALICE: I'm Alice Furlaud, in Paris.

THE DOG PRINCESS

This is not a creature from an ancient Egyptian frieze, but a French noblewoman with a Belgian title who owns and operates the best animal shelter in France. I first met Princess Elisabeth de Croÿ about thirty-five years ago in our apartment in Union Square, New York. That day she sat on our brand-new garbage can and permanently dented the lid. Elisabeth makes a permanent impression wherever she goes, especially in the world of animal welfare. But her shelter, the Refuge de Thiernay, where eighty to a hundred animals live in style waiting to be adopted, is anything but showy. It's way down a remote and bumpy dirt road, and living conditions for people are rudimentary. In the middle of one very cold winter night in Elisabeth's unheated farmhouse, I was persuaded to lend my precious hot-water bottle to a dying dog. The dog, in fact, lived—next day I got my hot-water bottle back, rather muddy.

You would never know from the following guided tour of the shelter that I had met most of the dogs several times before, and that on the unedited tape Elisabeth is constantly ordering me to "Turn off the machine!" while I keep asking her to "Say that again: the barking drowned you out." My "All Things Considered" piece started with a selection of barks of every timbre and style, with Elisabeth de Croÿ's melodious voice taking command of the pack.

(Dogs: yap-yap! Woof! Ruff! etc.)

PRINCESS: Loulou, you can't come in, you'll catch a chicken if you do. Loulou! Loulou! Loulou! *(Dog whines eagerly.)* Bouboule, tu veux venir? Bouboule! Viens, Bouboule! Bouboule! *(Miscellaneous yaps.)* One can sneak in to eat the cat food. *(Outraged yapping.)* Shh! Shh. Assez! Assez! Assez! *(Yap-yap-yap.)*

(Bouboule, the snarling, brindle-colored dog Elisabeth is trying to shut out of the cat wing here, was rescued from a sadistic master and is unsuitable for adoption because he bites any human being who approaches him — except Elisabeth de Croÿ. She can hug and even kiss him.)

ALICE: *(Narrating)* Princess Elisabeth de Croÿ's bark is a lot worse than her bite, especially when she's gently scolding her large personal retinue of "unadoptable" dogs. They always go with her on inspection tours of the three acres of enclosures for adoptable strays, and recent arrivals at the Refuge de Thiernay. The refuge is also the official animal protection society for the Department of the Nièvre. We stopped by the chalet of the fiercest dog in the shelter, a huge, red-eyed, black creature called Rock. The Princess single-handedly rescued Rock from solitary confinement and has been trying to tame him.

(Rock: full-throated, mastiff-type bark.)

PRINCESS: I did pat him once, but at the risk of my life. *(Rock growls.)* Rock! Rock! Rock! But you know, when a dog has been for nine months confined in a dark room, and the neighbor was kind enough to throw food through the broken window, the dog goes mad. *(Yap-yap-yapping from other dogs nearby.)*

ALICE: Now, how many dogs would you say are here right now?

PRINCESS: About fifty. I think you shouldn't have more, because you can't give them attention. What they do need is to go out and see things. Therefore we have no walls here. They can look at each other, they can snarl at each other, they can flirt with each other, they can see what's going on. Dogs have to be occupied! Their minds must see something! And trees! You see? They love trees. And they need grass. And in America they told me it was not hygienic to be on grass. *(Hysterical bark in the middle distance.)* You will notice two beautiful boxers. One belongs to the régisseur of the Lido — the stage director. He's going away; he couldn't keep him, and anyway, the dog didn't lead a very doggy life.

ALICE: *(Narrating)* The Princess started the shelter eighteen years ago with two legacies totalling about three thousand dollars. She says it just barely survives, on contributions from animal lovers as far away as Japan, plus most of her own income. There's a staff of four, but the Princess herself seems to be on duty twenty-four hours a day.

PRINCESS: This is the infirmary, where we give different injections and where we vaccinate the animals.

ALICE: And you do a lot of this yourself. Because I've seen you give an animal a fatal injection who was too badly wounded—

PRINCESS: Oh yes, you must do it immediately, you must not keep them suffering.

(In fact, it took not just one injection, but several, to put that dog "out of its misery," which had been caused by a car accident. In between shots, Elisabeth would hurry out of the alcove where the dog lay, panting, on thick layers of blankets, to deal with other emergencies. We had just arrived, after an afternoon of strenuous errands in Nevers. I crouched by the dog, a spanielesque mongrel with glassy, unseeing eyes, trying to remember thoughts from the Tibetan Book of the Dead. *Elisabeth was scornful of my sentimentality. I wasn't doing the dog any good, she said. I felt— and still feel—ashamed at the contrast between her twenty-four-hour-a-day, active compassion and my useless and intermittent sympathy.)*

ALICE: I've also seen you, at least heard you, in the middle of the night, answer a distress call, get into your ambulance yourself, go off on the roads. . . .

PRINCESS: There was a poor dog run over just the other side of Nevers. I went there but it was too late. She was still alive but she was unconscious.

ALICE: This is the veterinary wing. Oh, and here's a cat with all his toys.

ELISABETH: She came in yesterday. *(Cat miaows loudly.)* She's about two months old. Found her on the street. She's very lonely.

ALICE: She has a huge dish of milk she could drown in. *(Cat: Miaow!)*

ALICE: *(Narrating)* Fully-grown cats at the refuge are free either to stay in the barn, which is fitted up with ladders and cubbyholes and central heating, or to join the Princess and eight or ten dogs in her very unprincely little farmhouse across the dirt road from the shelter. At present about fifteen cats are in residence. Two of them have lost legs in farmers' traps; all are neutered, tattooed, and wearing the Refuge collar and tag. They lounge on the orange velvet chairs which Chopin used to sit on at the Princess's great-grandfather's house; they snooze on piles of important-looking documents and on photographs of important people.

PRINCESS: This is Rex Harrison, I went on a cruise with Rex Harrison.

ALICE: Where did you go?

PRINCESS: Capri. I mean there were other people also.

ALICE: And here you are with Indira Gandhi.

PRINCESS: Indira Gandhi, and there's another one with Kennedy. That was my English nurse, who was so wonderful. That was one of my first dogs, Gribouille; he was tied up with wire. He belonged to Algerians who burnt his head with cigarettes. But in fact he went to the Elysée once, but he had to wait in the car. It's quite true! I met General de Gaulle several times, but we didn't talk about his cat.

(*Time didn't permit a full description here of Elisabeth de Croÿ's living room and crisis center—the boxes of kitty litter lining the walls, the constant barking and scrambling, the constant ringing of the telephone, usually answered by the Princess before her secretary, in the office in the barn, could get to it. "You waited a week to report this dog missing?" she will chide a caller. "Was he tattooed? Et bien, that was a bad mistake, Monsieur. I am a mere volunteer here. Call during office hours tomorrow." To one of her helpers: "Shut that door! No cats in the kitchen!" And more gently to the dogs: "Someone has wee-weed here. Who is the cochon?" The serenity of even the newest-arrived of the cats, in the atmosphere created by this unserene highness, is one of Elisabeth's miracles. "She has a quality of Saint Francis about her," a retired English RSPCA official once told me.*)

ALICE: (Narrating) Her Serene Highness Princess Elisabeth de Cröy was born three miles from the shelter, in the Château d'Azy. She's one of seven sisters: all princesses, all animal lovers, and all living at least part of the time in or near the family castle. Elisabeth left home early to see the world, beginning as a TWA hostess in the days when the planes were Constellations. She did relief work in Africa during the Biafra famine; for years she drove regular truckloads of clothes and medicine to Poland, and she actively collects for Mother Teresa of Calcutta. But her main mission, to help animals, began when she was a little girl. She says she was obsessed by the suffering of animals in the countryside around her, such as farm dogs who were chained up all their lives.

PRINCESS: And I was traumatized once at a hunt when sixty hounds were chasing a wild boar, and I don't know how many people galloping on horseback. And I was put on a horse, and I couldn't bear the poor—I was on the side of the poor wild boar. So from then on I thought that one day I would really do all I could for animals.

ALICE: *(Narrating)* This summer the Princess's sister Mimi staged a local rock festival for the benefit of the refuge. Princess Mimi is a composer herself. In her old manor house near Thiernay she shelters not only two ancient mongrels and an attic full of owls, but occasional rock musicians. There's a recording studio complete with synthesizer, where Julian Lennon recorded the songs for his first album, naming it after Mimi's house, Valotte. One of Princess Mimi's songs in praise of Princess Elisabeth's good works is called "Elisabeth Loves Animals." *(Ambience: song for fifteen seconds, fading under following script:)* "Elisabeth loves animals, she takes care of animals, Bow wow wow, miaow. . ."

ALICE: *(Narrating)* The voices here are all Princess Mimi's, except for a few contributions from the residents of her sister's animal shelter. *(Fade up song.)* For National Public Radio, I'm Alice Furlaud, in Thiernay, France. *(Fade up song: I suggested that the best part comes just after the word* distress, *where there's a miserable howl.)*

Mimi de Croÿ's voice is huskier and lower in pitch than her sister's but she has overdubbed her voice in this song so that she sings both alto and soprano (not always in synch), with a basic rock continuo on the synthesizer. The song has an amazing array of dogs howling dismally, donkeys braying, birds tweeting, and Mimi herself doing a convincing miaow. Mimi, in her late fifties, was until recently a farmer, raising the white Charolais cattle of the region. She was dressed like a farmhand the day Elisabeth and I dropped in on her. She insisted on giving me a generous glass of unadulterated Southern Comfort while we sat listening to the tape of Mimi's sad voice amplified by speakers placed around the ancient honey-colored walls of her salon.

The scene seemed as fragile as a moth's wing: the goodness and the eccentricity of the sisters; their fierce, body-and-soul dedication to a cause; and the empty green hills seen through the old stone window.

TONNERRE ON THE RIGHT

Patricia Brett, reporting for Monitoradio, and I for NPR, were the only representatives of the English-speaking press at the youth conference organized by the hyper-right-wing presidential candidate, Jean-Marie Le Pen, in Strasbourg in 1988. You'd have thought that we would be small game for the Le Pen aides: two reporters from radio networks the National Front had never heard of, who spent an inordinate amount of time howling with laughter together in corners. But the staff treated us as if we were Woodward, Bernstein, Richard Harding Davis, Oriana Fallaci and the fox in the chicken coop, all rolled into one. I was surprised at their charming manners, though: normally in France, the attitudes of people in charge of the press range from unhelpful to sulky. But tweedy and jovial though the Le Pen men were, they never seemed to take their eyes off Pat and me for a minute. I'll admit we were something of a change from the French press, who seemed to me to be anything but inquiring in their attitude. They sat docilely around the press table at the banquet while Pat and I were swooping all over the room catching fascist songs and slogans with our microphones.

Pat kept after the Le Pen people for weeks after the conference, pointing out inconsistencies and evasions in their campaign literature, etc. At the election-night party in a tent in Le Pen's garden, we were treated with the respect usually accorded to Time or Newsweek. But it was Pat who got a Christmas card from the Le Pen staff—not me.

On "All Things Considered," the host, Robert Siegel, read the introduction to my first political feature.

HOST: One of the big surprises of these pre-election days in France is the popularity of the National Front, the extreme right-wing party led by the charismatic candidate Jean-Marie Le Pen. Attendance at his rallies is enormous, and in the polls he's running a close fourth — President Mitterand is the front-runner. Le Pen is not considered to be electable, but speculation is mounting about how he will direct his supporters to vote in the run-off election on May 8th. Recently he convened and financed a conference of right-wing youth from twenty-one European countries, in Strasbourg, where Alice Furlaud observed the fervor of Le Pen's campaign.

(Sound of Le Pen greeting an ecstatically cheering audience.)

LE PEN: Salut! Salut à vous, jeunes filles et jeunes gens d'Europe, venus aujourd'hui à Strasbourg! *(Cheers.)*

ALICE: *(Narrating)* With his flowing silver hair, his jutting lower lip, and his upper set gleaming in a broad smile, Jean-Marie Le Pen reminds you of Maurice Chevalier. And he can sing!

LE PEN: Allons, enfants de la patrie . . . *(A splendid a cappella rendition of the "Marseillaise.")*

ALICE: *(Narrating)* And this son of a Breton fisherman can also talk. He uses no notes, just prowls up and down the stage speaking naturally, but poetically, for two or three hours at a time. He promises to expel North Africans from France, subsidize mothers who stay home and have babies, bring back the death penalty, declare war on terrorists, segregate AIDS victims and beef up defense. The French, who adore their own language, *like* diatribes against immigrants to be expressed in faultless imperfect subjunctives and smothered in classical references. As, for instance, when Le Pen lists the various battles when Europeans turned back the Arab hordes, starting with the Greeks versus the Persians at Marathon.

LE PEN: Marathon! Salamin! Lépante! Vienne, et Poitiers! *(Vigorous applause.)*

ALICE: Le Pen is a deputy to the European Parliament, and by flying 500 young people from all over Europe to Strasbourg, at great expense, he's giving a European and a youthful dimension to his campaign. Jan Smits, a Dutch delegate, thinks the conference will help Europe, too.

JAN SMITS: *(a sober young woman)* I think what we do see in this convention is that the Front National movement in France is giving

127

birth to other nationalistic—in a good sense nationalistic—movements in the rest of Europe, which haven't felt free, or dared to exist, up to now.

ALICE: Seen en masse, the delegates, mostly young men wearing neckties and very short hair, looked like conscripts for a small war. Blue jeans were rare, and no one had a Walkman or jogging shoes. The two black people present turned out to be a TV cameraman and a photographer from *Gai Pied*, the Paris gay newspaper.

(Sound: young men's voices in revelry and song are heard under following narration:)

ALICE: At a banquet the first night in the old city, the traditional Alsatian sauerkraut was served with a lot of Alsatian Gewurztraminer wine. The Italians began singing an old Blackshirt song, and the Spaniards sang the Falangist song "Cora del Sol." *(Young men in a rather drunken chorus of this song, which sounds a little like a very militant version of "I've Been Working on the Railroad.")*

ALICE: Several arms were raised in the Fascist salute, and the Le Pen aides rushed over to these tables, gesturing to the pianist for help. One was heard to whisper, "Let's get rid of the journalists!" *(Meaning Pat and me!)* No one took him up on this, but they turned the lights off and played the "Marseillaise," the equivalent of "Good Night, Ladies" in France. *(Piano strikes up a wobbly rendition of the "Marseillaise," joined by even wobblier youths.)* So everybody had to leave before the coffee, and the London-based Russian delegates left the conference for good at this point, to protest the Fascist tone of the proceedings.

The friendly tone in which Le Pen spoke next day of the German role in World War II, brought loud applause from the young Europeans, and big headlines in the French press:

LE PEN: *(Before an admiring audience)* Ayons le courage de comprendre que certains n'eurent pas l'exclusivité des crimes, et les autres l'exclusivité du bon droit et de l'héroisme! *(Fades under narration.)*

ALICE: Speaking in front of the flags of all nations, Le Pen said no one side had had a monopoly of either criminal behavior or heroism. He spoke of the great empires of European history and urged the audience to build a new European empire in the twenty-first century.

LE PEN: D'Alexandre à Cesar, de Charlemagne à Hitler, de Napoléon à Staline . . .

ALICE: The plane carrying the French delegation from Paris to Strasbourg was two hours late because of a bomb threat. The television station F.R. 3, the only one to film the Fascist salutes at the dinner, had to be evacuated because of a bomb threat just before they broadcast it. And the day the conference ended, another bombshell appeared on the newsstands: the trendy magazine *Globe* had a cover story on Le Pen's ex-wife, Pierrette, with a picture of her tearing up a photograph of Le Pen with her teeth. Last year Pierrette, who's in her fifties, posed for *Playboy* with nothing on but a tiny maid's cap and apron. She claimed Le Pen had told her to get a job as a domestic servant.

Jobs are a major preoccupation in France, one which adds to the many different dissatisfactions of Le Pen's motley crowd of supporters. These include bourgeois industrialists, Communist workers, aristocrats, vast numbers of young people and, some say, a sprinkling of Moonies. None of them like the way the world is going. They're afraid of crime, prices, drugs, disease, and Arab immigration threatening their jobs. And this is the really dangerous bomb ticking away under the French nation: the unprecedented unemployment—10.5 percent of the active population. The explosion, if all those people should wake up on April 24th and start voting for Le Pen, could just possibly blow the structure of French political life to smithereens.

(Sound: a huge auditorium full of enthusiasts chanting "Vive Le Pen! Vive Le Pen!" in Nuremberg rally style.)

For National Public Radio, I'm Alice Furlaud, in Paris.

Before my sign-out was over, NPR had faded out the sinister shouts and substituted the wistful, romantic accordion music which always accompanies everything French on the radio.

RETURN OF THE GUILLOTINE

From the very first minute of 1989, France began celebrating the 200th anniversary of the French Revolution with such fervor that long before July 14th people were complaining they were sick and tired of the whole thing. Shop windows featured chess sets with royalty opposing sans-culottes, books about every single bit player in the events, pain révolutionnaire—"revolutionary bread" with 1789 burned into the crust, signs advertising "revolutionary prices" in red, white and blue (only the French say blue white and red), and guillotines everywhere, from life-size models to lapel pins. Everybody's getting into the act! Even S. S. Sakya Trinzin, who sailed into Paris the other day to speak about Tibetan Buddhism, sent out pamphlets which compare the "Outer Revolution of 1789" to the "inner revolution" of the Buddha.

There was a race among media people to track down direct descendants of Bastille attackers, executioners, Committee of Public Safety members, and knitters around the guillotine. I think I am the only one who found a direct descendant of Dr. Jean-Isaac Guillotin, the inventor of the guillotine. Dr. Guillotin was a physician who lived in a Paris house on the Rue St. Honoré, very near the Place de la Concorde where the guillotine did its grisly work. His descendant, Dr. C. Ira Guillotin, lives in a small apartment on the third floor (fourth floor as Americans count them) of that same house. All around the walls are glass-fronted shelves crammed with ancient-looking surgical instruments and other memorabilia and documents. Dr. Guillotin is in his sixties: tall, stooped and balding, with gold pince-nez. He reminds me a little of former President Valéry Giscard d'Estaing and has the same courteous, stately manner and strong French accent. But his eyes have the faraway gleam of the visionary. We sat on an old green velvet sofa, and Dr. Guillotin's first statement was a test for the correct sound level on my tape recorder. But I began my "All Things Considered" piece with it.

DR. GUILLOTIN: Docteur Guillotin, who invented the guillotine which was used in the French Revolution was my great-great-great-great-grandfather.

ALICE: And as I understand it he was born in this very house that we're standing in.

DR. GUILLOTIN: No, no, no! Docteur Guillotin was born in Aix en Provence. He came to live here when he was about twenty-seven years old, it was a property he acquired through marriage. And I myself was born here.

ALICE: Well, it's a wonderful, wonderful house, and he invented the guillotine right here, in this house?

DR. GUILLOTIN: He invented it in a small workshop in a house that belonged to the concierge on the other side, but it was here that he was living, and his workshop was over there. If you like to see, this was his office and this (*Opens obviously heavy French windows with a squeak of the handle; loud traffic sounds come up from below*) was the view that he had, you know, down to your left 200 yards. Yes! This is the Rue St. Honoré, you see?

ALICE: Yes . . .

DR. GUILLOTIN: The people were coming to have their heads cut off, and they would come down from the prison on the Ile de la Cité and they would come up here, you see? In those days the Rue St. Honoré was a two-way street, now it is one way that way, but in the other times they used to come this way, and then of course they came and they had this beautiful, beautiful view, they came up through what is now, of course, the Hotel Crillon, right next to your embassy, the American Embassy, and there in the middle of the Place de la Concorde in the most beautiful possible site they were—well, they were guillotined! Ha-ha-ha-ha . . .(*Dr. Guillotin's loud laugh is mirthful, but has an edge to it.*)

ALICE: And all these cases: are these full of his things?

DR. GUILLOTIN: These are very rare drawings. Very old sketches. You see, there they're tripping the guillotine!

131

ALICE: These are actual drawings that Dr. Guillotin himself drew?

DR. GUILLOTIN: No, that one is by his mother. This is his picture of the original foundry which was in fact in Germany where the blades, where the family first had the blades made; since the nineteenth century we've been doing them in Clermont Ferrand.

ALICE: Oh, in other words the family continued to have this sort of concession of guillotines, and make them.

DR. GUILLOTIN: If you'll excuse the phrase, we have been getting royalties! And look! Look! Here, you see, in that wax picture, under the wax that is the hair of Charlotte Corday.

ALICE: Oh! Let me see now, could we hold that up to the light, because it's a – oh my goodness.

DR. GUILLOTIN: You see, it's absolutely priceless and beautifully preserved, although actually her hair was red.

ALICE: It's not actually bloody, is it?

DR. GUILLOTIN: Oh, no, I don't think so. If it were bloody it would be black.

ALICE: Isn't that fascinating! Now, how did he come to invent it? I mean I'm most interested in how – I mean, he was a doctor.

DR. GUILLOTIN: Yes, but I would like to talk to you about me. I, too, am Docteur Guillotin. Now since the arrival of President Mitterand there is no more guillotine in France because capital punishment is temporarily suspended. But – well! Come with me. I want to show you something that is really interesting, I think, I *think*. Watch out for the step! *(Slam! Door closes. A whooshing sound is heard.)* Excuse me, I was turning off the suction side pump. And here it is!

ALICE: What do you mean, it. Oh! Excuse me. *(Flabbergasted.)*

DR. GUILLOTIN: You are the first person of your radio company to see the guillotine of tomorrow.

ALICE: What do you mean? Now wait, now . . .

DR. GUILLOTIN: The guillotine of the second millennium, which I hope will be some day seen internationally, all over the world.

ALICE: This is *your* invention?

DR. GUILLOTIN: It is my life work. Even when I was a student at your Massachusetts Institute of Technology I was thinking of this.

ALICE: My gosh, it takes up the whole room. It's a sort of gaping fishlike machine, it's as big as a Volkswagen.

DR. GUILLOTIN: Attendez, I'll turn it on. *(Sound: a computerish peeping sound mixed with occasional thuds as of a giant onion chopper. But the sound has outer-spacelike vibrations, a feeling of E. T. calling home.)*

DR. GUILLOTIN: It is laser operated and electronically controlled.

ALICE: Oh!

DR. GUILLOTIN: The work can be done by any almost inexperienced technician. This here is a side suction pump which will take the laser blade and it will come and then, you see? Look, look, *look!* . . . Absolutely painless.

ALICE: Oh . . . this is where the person puts their head? I didn't quite see, because the laser . . .

DR. GUILLOTIN: No, non, non. That is where the head is, just before it goes in the little plastic bag. *That* is where the body is just before it goes in the *big* plastic bag.

ALICE: *(Breathlessly)* Oh my gosh . . .

DR. GUILLOTIN: And these are automatically sealed with the name of the person and everything other information which is to acquire is put directly into the microchip.

ALICE: It says "laser" on that door. If you open it—may I—

DR. GUILLOTIN: *(Very upset)* Oh! NO! NO! *(Calming himself with an effort.)* It's perfectly safe, but just to be sure.

ALICE: You mean I could have had my head cut off? *(Nervous giggle.)*

DR. GUILLOTIN: Yes. No! No, no, no, but there's no reason to take any chances.

ALICE: I'm really quite surprised. I mean, this may come into actual use in your lifetime?

DR. GUILLOTIN: I think this will become again a household name, not only in France but in many European countries and

Francophone Africa—perhaps even in certain American states. *(Dr. Guillotin laughs his, by now, rather sinister laugh.)*

ALICE: For National Public Radio, I'm Alice Furlaud in Paris.

This feature was an April Fool piece for "All Things Considered." It seems to have fooled quite a few people until the very end when I admitted it was a "poisson d'avril." The part of Dr. Guillotin was played by Max—entirely ad-lib. My gasps of amazement in the broadcast were genuine, as I never knew what he was going to say.

CAPE COD PESTS

This piece aired on "All Things Considered," Thanksgiving 1987.
Europe is a wonderful place to learn about things that I never knew
about America. It was the Austrian Count Arnold Keyserling, who
has a great white beard and a castle, who first initiated me into some
of the mystical mysteries of the American Indians—he had just come
back from the Indian prairies where he'd learned the Secrets of the
Grandfathers. I had my first sweat lodge with the Cherokee Indian
Swift Deer of Los Angeles on the grounds of a French château. We
sat in a wigwam around a huge heap of red-hot stones from the château
courtyard with a lot of naked, sweaty French people invoking the
Great Spirit and Mother Earth. "O Grand Esprit, Mère Terre . . ." (This
was a place where no tape recorder could follow without fear of melt-
down.) But I can't say that I keep up with the latest American trends.
Even if you come back twice a year, the changes on the home scenes
seem immense.

The price of land on Cape Cod, for instance, appears to shoot up
every day, almost as fast as the supply of space and drinking water
shoots down. The national park took over a lot of Cape Cod twenty
years ago, and what's left of this fragile little hook off Massachusetts
is under tremendous pressure from builders, developers and members
of the vacationing human race—to the chagrin of some of the mem-
bers of certain other races, both human and not, who live in Cape
Cod year-round.

ALICE: (*Over hammering*) Every time I come home to Cape Cod—
whether I've been away for a month or six months—there's a
kaleidoscopic change in the landscape. You close your eyes, open
them and there it is, right on your doorstep! A new mall or a lobster

pizza takeout, or some neighbor who's divided a beautiful red huckle-berry hill into bite-sized portions. As winter gets nearer there's a regular plague of hammering and cement mixing. And along with *this* plague has come a plague of mice.

My mother's barn, which used to be a guest house, is occupied by a colony of white-footed field mice. They've found out that nobody is ever there in the winter, and this is because a year ago the fur-nace broke down and blew a thick coating of oil up into the house. I can't understand why our government seems to want to fight a war over oil. Oil is ghastly, especially when it's all over your arm-chairs and quilts and pictures. Oil should be banned, not defended by our battleships in the Persian Gulf or anywhere *else*! Anyway, my mother and I have taken right against the stuff and have not replaced the furnace. So now that the coast is clear, the mouse guests have moved in and made themselves cozy nests out of things like boxes of old family letters and the stuffing from teddy bears. They've found that there's nourishing protein in the red leather bindings of a set of Dickens, and they are not housetrained. My mother's old cat is no help. Outdoors, this giant cat is known to the chip-munks as the Terminator. But he doesn't believe in hunting indoors. He'll sit with folded arms watching a mouse scuttle across the floor as if it were a wind-up toy.

I hate traps and poisons, but in the Yellow Pages I found Mr. Barney Pearce, of AA Animal and Pest Control, 7 Days a Week, Humane Methods, down in Harwich. Mr. Pearce is a pest controller whose sympathies are entirely with the pests. On the telephone he told me field mice are *flocking* into old houses this year. "It's this crazy building boom," he said. "It's driving all the poor mice and voles and shrews on to undisturbed ground. These little fellas have got to go somewhere!" Mr. Pearce clearly feels with Walt Whitman that "a mouse is miracle enough to stagger sextillions of infidels." With awe he described how a field mouse can flatten its head to get through a crack just wide enough for a human fingernail. He advised me to buy a harmless trap called a Tin Cat. You collect mice in this and then drive them six miles away and release them. He agreed, sadly, that this might separate some mouse families forever.

The real pests on Cape Cod are the real estate profiteers, all hastening to get their developments and condominiums built before clean water laws put a stop to them. They're like field mice scrabbling for cover before the winter comes, only much more destructive. If only Barney Pearce would put on his Pied Piper suit and pipe all these human pests away, from Provincetown right down to the Cape Cod Canal, I'd put up with the mice. After all, their ancestors were here when the *Mayflower* sailed into Cape Cod Bay, just about this time of year.

TOUGH, BUT OH, SO GENTLE

My trip to Geneva with the French team competing in the Monsieur Monde contest was one of the jolliest happenings in my radio life. I first met this group of bodybuilders in their Paris gym, flexing their "abs" and their "traps." I was with them on a hilarious train ride to Switzerland and in our rather scruffy Geneva hotel, and out of pure, wide-eyed fascination spent more hours with them day after day in the contest hall than the mere story I wrote for the International Herald Tribune *and my radio feature for Deutsche Welle could possibly justify. These muscle people—all black—were the friendliest bunch of French citizens I had ever met. If only so many of the contestants had not chosen the* Chariots of Fire *music for their poses!*

HOST: *(For Deutsche Welle)* The city of Geneva should be used to almost anything in the way of international conferences by now. But earlier this month a conspicuously brawny group caused Genevan heads to turn on the streets and lakeshores: the World Amateur Body Building Association was in town. They were meeting to decide which of 150 muscle men from forty-one countries should win the title of Mr. World—or Monsieur Monde—1983. As the bodybuilders headed for Geneva, Alice Furlaud muscled in on their act.

(Sound: Chariots of Fire *music and loud clapping fades under.)*

CRAIG MUNSON: *(Sounds a little like Mohammed Ali)* Compete in Europe, you know? Come to Europe. The people will love you! Train hard, come to Europe, they said. So I'm here!

ALICE: *(Narrating)* Craig Munson, an absolute mountain of a man, has come to Switzerland from Los Angeles. And Colette Le

138

Hémoneau has come from Paris, with a railroad car of other bodybuilding groupies.

COLETTE: French people love bodybuilding. They have to support their friends and their champions. You have to shout the name of the one you want to win.

SUPPORTER: *(Hoarse but enthusiastic, slight French accent)* John Brown! John Brown! John Brown!

(Sound: Chariots of Fire *music played slowly, with reverent clapping at intervals, heard under following:)*

ALICE: On stage in the Geneva Palexpo, a big new exhibition hall near the airport, Mr. Sadek of Egypt, in a red bikini, is doing his posing routine to the music he, and just about every other contestant, has chosen. He's shaved all over and gleaming with oil so that his muscles will catch the light just right. He's moving in postures which range in style from ancient Greek discus thrower to modern disco. With each pose he switches on, or pops out, a different set of enormous muscles: his midriff looks like a relief map of the Himalayas.

Bodybuilding is new in Europe—but it's already a world with its own heroes—Brown, Kawak, Nubret—and it has its own language. Europeans like to use the original American words:

SHARON: He's not cut enough, he's not ripped enough, he's not dry enough!

ALICE: *(From the seat next to Sharon in the Palexpo)* You mean the muscles aren't defined?

SHARON: Ah! Watch him! The back view's a little better.

ALICE: It's useful to sit next to an expert. Sharon Boyle, an aerobics teacher from West Hollywood, is touring the European bodybuilding scene. She makes Jane Fonda look like Winnie-the-Pooh.

SHARON: That member of the French *équipe*, he's fifth from the end. You notice the difference? And also the one next to him, in the red? Gorgeous! Bookends. How would you like them as a pair of bronze bookends?

ALICE: All the real movement in this sport is done behind the scenes in a gym, where the builder uses machines and weights to isolate and enlarge specific muscles. This sounds like a healthy activity. Bob Jodkiewicz, one of the top professional contestants in Geneva, has been a bodybuilder ever since he was voted Mr. Teenage Brooklyn thirteen years ago:

BOB: (*Over the clinking and murmuring of the Geneva bar where we are sitting*) Right now I'm delirious. I really am. I'm dizzy and tired. (*Sighs.*) No glucose, blood sugar very low. See, your brain is not being fed. You can't think right, you start to hallucinate.

ALICE: (*Narrating*) That's the price of cutting out liquids and fats to get into show trim. Then there are steroids, male hormones which create instant muscle, but can cause liver damage and sterility—and also make the athlete quite goofy. Lots of European professionals admit to using these drugs, but they say it's only because the other guys did it first—an argument people are using at the medium-range missile negotiations a few blocks away.

Amateur bodybuilders supposedly do not use steroids. The amateurs here are apparently the ones who are *not* out in the lobby in intermission selling protein powder and pictures of themselves. Among the amateurs are the women candidates for Mademoiselle Monde—Miss World. There are no American contestants, perhaps because they think European standards for Miss Muscle World are too fluffy.

SERGE NUBRET: I like a woman who look feminine. I think in America a lot of bodybuilders just look for mass and size in women. But it's not good for a woman to show muscle, triceps like that.

ALICE: Serge Nubret has set the style for European women bodybuilders. He's a courtly Frenchman from Guadeloupe. At forty-five, he's not only a contestant here for Mr. World, but the organizer of the contest. He owns a large Paris gym and publishes a magazine called *Muscle Flash*. His own muscles are nearer movie-star than side-show proportions. And so are those of the females on the French team, headed by Serge.

SERGE NUBRET: She must be small waist, nice shape, not like a man, where you see all the veins.

140

ALICE: The winner of Miss World this year, the present Miss Germany, conforms to Nubret's specifications, to the disgust of Sharon Boyle.

SHARON: She's like most of the girls we saw today—they look like the cupcakes you see perched on a fender in an auto trade show. They even wore high heels!

ALICE: Mary Scott, this year's Miss Universe, who only placed fourth in Geneva, thinks the judges' standards are a bit vague.

MARY SCOTT: *(In a heavy Scottish accent)* Those girls that did not put their feet together should have been made to put their feet together. And all I can say is, those girls that did not put their feet together have something to hide. And they've hidden it!

ALICE: The judges came under heavier and heavier fire from disappointed fans as the awarding of the Mr. World trophy got closer.

ANNOUNCER: Classé deuxieme, représentant la France, Eduardo Kawak! *(Announcement nearly drowned out by Kawak supporters' jeers, whistles, insults.)*

ALICE: Eduardo Kawak, a Lebanese of twenty-three who is already Mr. Universe this year, has thigh muscles so huge they sort of overflow his actual leg. He's furious at being only runner-up, so he has grabbed the microphone to protest Serge Nubret's becoming Mr. World 1983.

KAWAK: Ladies and gentlemen, please for all the newspapers here, don't write that! I am the conqueror here! I thank you very much!

ALICE: *(Barely audible under the furious jeers of Kawak fans, near the judges' table up front)* A beleaguered judge, Jim Charles from England, defended the decision.

JIM CHARLES: Listen, I'm just one man with one honest opinion. I'm respected by the bodybuilding world in America, Germany, France or wherever you like. I'm an outspoken guy. I'm—what do you call it?

ALICE: A monster?

JIM CHARLES: An extrovert. It's got me in a lot of trouble and I've been suspended, but it doesn't matter, I give my honest opinion and

I'm respected. I don't want you to like me, just to respect my decision. *(More jeers and catcalls.)*

ALICE: But the wildest popular revolt was in favor of a totally unknown amateur, Craig Munson of Los Angeles, who came in sixth. No one needed a judge to see that Craig was by far the biggest builder in the contest. The crowd just wouldn't let him go, so he stayed onstage beaming and flexing away. *(Crowd cheering, clapping.)* Finally a judge came up and gave him a big, gaudy trophy with a red light and a statue on top—probably a consolation prize kept ready in the wings in case somebody had a tantrum. *(Sound: wild gabbling of Munson fans in lobby.)* Out in the lobby, Craig had the biggest crowd around him of anyone in the show.

CRAIG: I love the people here. The people are beautiful! They thought I would walk offstage and go back home, but the people here showed them no. The people chose their own! I'm a hairdresser. I do hair. I had to set a lot of appointments real early and real late in the evening, and make a lot of house calls, so I could get my workouts in.

ALICE: You've got hands the size of double baseball mitts!

CRAIG MUNSON: Double baseball mitts, and twenty-three-inch arms.

ALICE: Do I get to feel a bicep?

CRAIG MUNSON: Yes. Feel that!

ALICE: Gosh, it's like—the Alps! *(Clapping and shouting from crowd, who are pressing close around us.)*

CRAIG MUNSON: Next time the people see me I'll be much bigger!

ALICE: And before some European makes the inevitable complaint that Americans always have to be the biggest wherever they go, I'm Alice Furlaud, in Geneva.

C'EST MAGNIFIQUE, MAIS CE N'EST
PAS LA GARE!

HOST: *(For "All Things Considered")* The Museum of the Jeu de Paume, the favorite hangout of art-minded American tourists, is closed for the next two years, and its great collection of French Impressionist paintings has left and is never coming back. They've all been taken over to Paris's new museum of nineteenth-century art, the Musée d'Orsay, which opens next week. The building that houses the new museum is an art object itself. It's a large and imposing old railroad station, the Gare d'Orsay, which shut down years ago, but still dominates the Left Bank of the Seine. The museum's opening is the last great Paris art event of 1986. Alice Furlaud and a few hundred other journalists got in to see the Musée even before the president of France.

ALICE: *(Ad-libbing)* This museum isn't trying to forget it used to be a railroad station. At the end of this huge main hall with its glass barrel roof, there's the big gilt station clock—it's about the size of a swimming pool up there, and every once in a while on the loudspeaker there's one of those incomprehensible announcements they're always making in stations. *(Distant loudspeaker voice announces inaudible events.)* And here I am on a stone bench remembering when I last came into the Gare d'Orsay on a train. I spent the night here in the station hotel upstairs. Only now I'm looking through some modern marble portals over there at Manet's painting, *Le Déjeuner sur l'Herbe*. That's the picture that shocked Paris tremendously when it was painted in 1863, because in it a naked lady is having a picnic with two fully dressed men—they're even wearing their hats. And the new architecture of this museum is sort of a nice shock. They've lined this long, long, long room with freestanding stark slabs of

143

marble of different colors. The effect is sort of a Hollywood version of an Egyptian mausoleum. It's not finished, I mean there are lots of workmen wheeling wheelbarrows around and sawing things, and to find the pictures you have to go behind these marble slab walls into the nooks and corridors and up staircases and bridges placed among the old, flowery nineteenth-century iron work. But before I go off in search of *Whistler's Mother* – she's actually supposed to be here somewhere – I'm going to try and find Monsieur Rigaud, who's the president of this museum and one of the people who dreamed up the idea of changing the station into a museum.

(Sound: footsteps on marble floors, workmen shouting to each other and moving heavy objects.)

RIGAUD: It was a railway station. We have a duty of truth in architecture and in museums: it *was* a railway station. And it's obvious. Our problem was to magnify this architecture of Lalou, which is completely *mad* – Lalou was the architect of the Gare d'Orsay – and nevertheless to manage spaces and all necessary to show paintings and furniture and sculpture.

ALICE: *(Narrating)* To Jacques Rigaud the station itself is the principal nineteenth-century work of art on display. But groping my way around the new, forbidding marble passages, I missed the cozy little Jeu de Paume museum. Even with all the crowds, looking at the pictures there was like seeing them in somebody's living room. Assistant Curator Marc Bascou thinks they're better off here at the Musée d'Orsay.

MARC BASCOU: Cézanne was just on the staircase at the Jeu de Paume, and now at last there's a whole room just for Cézanne by itself, which is wonderful: something which never happened in Paris before!

ALICE: I never found that room, even after a serious study of the museum's map, which was like an architect's blueprint. The Impressionists seem to be up in an attic somewhere, and not all together. But finding things in French institutions is always a challenge. The ladies' room was just as hard to find as Cézanne, and the plumbing was *very* nineteenth century. *(Sound: old-fashioned cascading flush.)* But what you simply can't miss at the Musée d'Orsay are the great, imposing paintings and sculptures by the mid-nineteenth-century academic artists: the people the Impressionists were rebelling against, who are always thought of as the Bad Guys. Everywhere you look on the ground floor there are paintings by people like Courbet of sheep coming home at dusk, or oxen going to work at dawn: simple subjects like that, on canvasses the size of Cinemascope screens. The principal sculptor out in the main hall is *not* Rodin, although his *Balzac* can be seen peering over a balcony in his voluminous white plaster bathrobe. The featured sculptor is Jean- Baptiste Carpeaux, who did the great group of dancers on the front of the Paris Opera. His statues of celebrities and mythological heroes and animals are all over the place here, and they have an expansive energy and grand-ness which seems like the very spirit of the French nineteenth century.

And not only French. There are photographs by Lewis Carroll, and a window by Louis Tiffany, and I found a lovely portrait of a Spanish dancer by Sargent all by itself, in a room overlooking the river that had been left just the way it was in 1900: a nice, rest-ful riot of gilt, ormulu and cupids. *Whistler's Mother* deserves a room like this. But when I finally found her, she was hung on an austere stone wall. She's called *La Mère* here, of course. And Assistant Cura-tor Marc Bascou explained that she has been transferred here from the Louvre.

MARC BASCOU: One thing that is interesting for us is to look at works of art that we've known for years in a different setting. This one has been cleaned; it has this very subtle grey paint all over it, and it had a yellowish varnish over it which gave a wrong idea of the painting. It had to be pure grey with this gilt frame, which is the original frame, I think it's designed by Whistler. It's the frame he liked.

ALICE: Do French people like this picture?

MARC BASCOU: Oh yes, it's very popular here.

ALICE: Do you think Whistler's mother ever came into the Gare d'Orsay on a train?

MARC BASCOU: That would have been fun. Why not? *(Laughs indulgently.)*

(Sound: an old steam train puffing slowly into a station.)

ALICE: *(Narrating)* The aim of Paris's new museum is apparently to give art lovers a new perspective on the nineteenth century. Maybe it can give everybody a new perspective on old railroad stations, so many of which are lost and gone forever. If they ever do away with trains entirely, let's keep New York's Grand Central Station and Washington's Union Station and fill them up with pictures. For National Public Radio, I'm Alice Furlaud, in Paris. *(Fade up whoo-whoo and chug-chug of train.)*

ART AND SUFFERING IN NINETEENTH-CENTURY PARIS

We foreign free-lances all love working in the lavish Boston studios of Monitoradio and basking in the lavish compliments of the staff. But after a while I began to feel shades of censorship close around me. You couldn't mention cigarettes, wine, cannibalism, hospitals, doctors, and a whole range of gloomy or cruel subjects. They were so pleasant and positive about it all, though, that it hardly seemed an intrusion: like Montessori nursery-school teachers, they sweetly diverted you to something else.

Confrontation finally came over—what else?—Van Gogh's ear. For my feature on the Van Gogh show at the Musée d'Orsay, I recorded a lot of sound from the movie Lust for Life. I used the turmoily music from the ear scene, ending with Kirk Douglas's ghastly scream, to run underneath my reference to "the torment inside the painter which led him to cut off his ear." I was asked to leave the ear part out. I could see that maybe the scream was overdoing it a bit, but I maintained that you could not write about Van Gogh without saying he cut off his ear. Steve Webbe, the producer, stood his ground, resisting the words cut off not because of Christian Science teaching, he maintained, but because part of the ear remained, so cut off was inaccurate. I told him I found this reasoning devious, but after a valiant fight I had to accept his word mutilate, which I thought much creepier than cut off, suggesting punks with safety pins in their ears.

I also wasn't allowed to say that Van Gogh had a "creative soul." Steve wanted soul changed to genius. I sneakily recorded the phrase with the word spirit and hoped Steve wouldn't notice. We are still very good friends.

For "All Things Considered" I wrote a commentary on the Van Gogh and Degas shows, which opened simultaneously on opposite

*sides of the Seine. I sent them some old-fashioned, nostalgic barrel
organ music to start the piece. Then:*

ALICE: The old movie *Lust for Life* is playing at the Musée d'Orsay
along with the "Van Gogh in Paris" exhibition. At one point Vincent Van Gogh, played by Kirk Douglas, says, "Maybe I never should
of come to Pairuss." He couldn't have been more wrong. During
his two years in Paris, from 1886 to 1888, Vincent changed from
a Dutch painter of gloomy colors into a vivid, glowing French Impressionist. He saw all the new pictures in town and tried all the styles.
He painted with blobs like the old Impressionists, and he painted
with dots like the new Impressionists, and he painted realistically
and orientally and academically. He painted the bridges over the
Seine and all the Montmartre windmills, and the insides and out-
sides of cafés, and lovely country views in suburbs of Paris that are
now polluted slums.

This show includes lots of other young painters who were doing
the same scenes—maybe sitting on camp stools next to Vincent's.
Painters like Signac and Bernard and Seurat. And for those of us
who identify Vincent with the last years in Arles, and all the fiery
yellow colors and going crazy and cutting off his ear, his brief life
as a Paris artist sitting around in cafés with friends is a revelation,
along with the unknown paintings in this show.

One Paris painter Van Gogh admired but never met was Edgar
Degas. He didn't hang around the cafés of Montmartre. He hung
around the grand salons of the day and the elegant boxes at the
elegant race courses and, of course, backstage at the ballet. There
are more than 300 pictures and statues in his exhibit, and it takes
a whole afternoon to file past the austere family groups and the horses
and jockeys and dancers and women taking baths in tiny tin tubs.
Staggering out of the Grand Palais, I had an oppressive feeling about
Degas' nineteenth-century pre-Eiffel Tower Paris. Van Gogh painted
it so joyfully! The one sad Van Gogh painting, three pairs of worn-
out boots, is so lit from within with love and feeling for the very
poor, I was in tears—uplifting tears.

Because Van Gogh was in touch with the core and meaning of
life, while between Degas and the poor women he painted in the
brothels and hat shops and ballet schools of Paris, I sense a screen
of stiff, macho attitudes. All those men in dark, formal morning
coats and black top hats lounging around the theaters or the races!

They make a sort of sinister background to the whole exhibit. Even in the Degas portraits of the painters Renoir and Manet and the avant-garde poet Mallarmé, they're wearing these forbidding clothes. So did Degas, of course, when he drew all those splendid pictures of nudes and prostitutes and those exhausted laundresses – the women who had to starch and iron all those white dress shirts. And suddenly I see Degas through my own screen of feminist outrage. Why couldn't they iron their *own* dress shirts? Why aren't there any *men* struggling to bathe in those miserable flat tubs? And as for the endless pastels of weary young ballerinas, Degas seems to me to draw them with the contempt of a bored boulevardier.

There is, in fact, one picture where Degas seems to feel on equal terms with his female subject: it's of the American Impressionist painter Mary Cassatt looking at a painting in the Louvre. Degas and "Mees Cassatt," as all the French artists called her, were good friends. I felt they did go to the Louvre together that day, and that her tightly laced figure, seen from behind leaning on her umbrella, was sketched with comradely affection.

(Sound: the elegant hubbub of the Café de la Paix.)

Recovering at the Café de la Paix, a gaudy place which Degas probably knew well and which Van Gogh never could have afforded, I wonder: why do I so resent this brilliant artist Degas? Maybe because he seems to paint the cruel life of nineteenth-century Paris so unsympathetically; maybe because Degas was revered as a painter in his long, opulent life, while Van Gogh sold only two pictures in his short, straitened life. Maybe because I think of Van Gogh as "Vincent," while I wouldn't dare to call Degas "Edgar." The fact is, it's a hundred years since Degas and Van Gogh overlapped in Paris, and now both the black-coated man-about-town and the inspired lunatic have become luxury consumer goods. Give or take a few million dollars at the auction block, they're both equal now. For National Public Radio, I'm Alice Furlaud, in Paris.

My nineteenth-century barrel organ tune was supposed to come up after that sign-out. I'd recorded this in Toulouse, where an ancient organ grinder was making a whole pedestrian street sound like the nineteenth century. But at the last minute, when getting the commentary ready for the air, an NPR technical genius spotted that the tune came from the movie Mary Poppins. So they quickly substituted something else. If the ear-cutting sounds from Lust for Life were the wrong background for Van Gogh, how about "Just a Spoonful of Sugar Makes the Medicine Go Down?"

149

A LA MODE

I rarely report on the Paris fashion scene. The modern dress shows in huge tents with their thumping rock music, flashing cameras and strange fashion groupies, half of whom seem to be young, unshaven men dressed in cruel-looking outfits, depress me. But then so did the old haute couture openings I occasionally attended in the late 1940s, in the hushed salons of Balmain or Grès, with the haughty ladies in the front row and the death penalty for anyone caught making a sketch. But as no book with Paris as the main character should leave out fashion, I include my NPR "Morning Edition" feature on what I'm sure was the weirdest fashion year of the century—1985.

HOST: The Paris prêt-à-porter, or ready-to-wear, fashion collections have just been unveiled, and never have they caused more excited comment. The new clothes are bizarre, but they're big business: France's second-biggest export after military weapons. Alice Furlaud has been investigating the odder aspects of the Paris mode scene.

(Music: Dionne Warwick's "Track of the Cat," complete with jungle noises, tigers growling, etc., fading under script.)

ALICE: *(Narrating)* All year the new outrageous designers have been marshalling their forces outside the Paris establishment, causing the capital to quake with fear. And when the ready-to-wear collections opened all over Paris, these bad guys moved in and took possession of the city. The Japanese designer Kimijima had his models stalk through the ornate, gilded ballroom of the Grand Hotel dressed as Nicaraguan guerrillas, complete with Castro camouflage caps, khaki lace see-through miniskirts and bras, and Kalashnikov machine guns: literally dressed to kill. Another set of Kimijima girls carried spears and wore skin-tight dresses with their faces painted to match in abstract patterns of black, brown, and white, imitating the body paint of the Sudanese Nuaros tribe.

But the real No-More-Mr.-Nice-Guy of French fashion is Jean-Paul Gaultier. Far out even geographically, his show was in a cavernous covered market in a Paris suburb. Down the runway came an endless funeral procession of dark, angry costumes worn by male and female models with furious frowns and aggressive slouches. *(Slouchy music is heard under this.)* There were men with shaved heads, bare to the waist, and wearing long, tight black skirts with mermaid fins. Others had long, matted hair and dinner jackets with no shirts on underneath. The women all had crocheted totem poles attached to their heads, uneven hemlines and backpacks. And the enthusiastic audience *(Wild clapping)* who crammed the huge building to the rafters were also dressed in ferocious flea-market fashions. Sasha, an assistant fashion designer, all in black with a pigtail down his back, definitely had the look, or *le look*, as they all say here.

ALICE: *(On location)* Could you describe to me what you're wearing?

SASHA: I'm wearing a . . .

ALICE: Gaucho?

SASHA: Normal pants, and there is just a little half a skirt behind me, so . . .

ALICE: There's a sort of a kilt ruffle attached to the back of the trousers.

SASHA: That's it! *(Giggles.)* A very little black jacket, with . . .

ALICE: A sort of a big shawl collar . . .

SASHA: That's right. It's for the winter.

ALICE: You've got a sort of a Sabu pigtail.

SASHA: It's a little Spanish line, like a toreador. *(Laughs gamely.)*

ALICE: Sasha, what is different this very year, about the whole fashion picture? It seems to be exploding somehow.

SASHA: Yeah. It's two years now that it's changing, you know? Because now people can wear everything, you can mix everything with everything.

ALICE: You mean I can even wear *this?*

SASHA: *(After a brief, appalled silence)* Yes! Why not? Because what's important now is just le look: that people see that you have made an effort to put some things on.

ALICE: *(Narrating over clapping)* Long ago, somebody said that fashion is a way of not having to decide who you really are. Sasha says today's fashion is an important way of expressing who you are: a total necessity for his generation.

SASHA: The world is beginning to be harder and harder now. And you have to express yourself, because if you're not expressing you, you will be—pushed down.

ALICE: *(Narrating)* I asked Nathalie, the one girl at the show not dressed in combined punk and grandmother's-trunk style, what she thought of the Gaultier collection.

NATHALIE: *(Over background sound of Gaultier fashion freaks)* I don't know—it's a mixture.

ALICE: How would you describe it?

NATHALIE: In English, I can't! *(Gales of laughter.)*

ALICE: *(Narrating)* But it was the baddest boy of Paris fashion, Azzedine Alaya, who won French television's brand-new award, the Oscar for Best Designer of the Year. Azzedine is the Tunisian newcomer, slightly over four feet tall and unheard-of two years ago, who snatched his collection away from Bergdorf Goodman's the other day, when they refused to fly his eighteen assistants and his dog to New York on the Concorde.

Azzedine's show took place in relays in a small, tightly packed studio. Wearing skirts so tight you could almost hear the seams ripping, and showing flesh where you'd least expect to see it, Azzedine's models coiled down the runway like cobras. Their clothes were somber, muddy, and sulky, and they were worn without jewels, hats, or handbags. Was it also part of le look, I asked Azzedine afterwards, to have no music? After all, he used to design clothes for the Folies Bergères!

ALAYA: Demain on aura de la musique.

ALICE: "Tomorrow we'll have music," he promised, enigmatically. I also asked him if his wide-shouldered, heavy-pocketed leather jackets weren't a bit too hot for, say, the New York summer. He denied this indignantly:

ALAYA: Non, non, c'est pas chaud du tout!

ALICE: *(Narrating over crowd chatter)* But whether or not he and the other avant-garde designers want to roast, constrict, or insult their customers, it's hard to know by whom and where all these garments will be worn next spring. Nathalie wondered too.

NATHALIE: *(Also in crowd)* There are not many people who can wear that kind of dress. It's expensive and strange, and you can't work in an office wearing this kind of clothes. It's impossible. So I wonder when people can wear that kind of clothes. I can't understand, really! I'm twenty years old, but I can't understand!

(Sinister rock version of the "Marseillaise" fades under sign-out.)

ALICE: For National Public Radio, I'm Alice Furlaud, in Paris, wearing a grey flannel suit and sensible shoes.

153

MAN'S INHUMANITY TO MAN
AND EVERYBODY ELSE

The phrase *human rights* is being flung around these days more recklessly than ever before. And if I were a mole, or a rat, or a badger, or a toad, I would resent its elitist implications. The only right that I can think of that doesn't belong to our fellow animals is copyright. It's because animals are the *real* silent majority, unable to express their wisdom in any form acceptable to human society, that animal rights agitators should stop planting bombs in research labs and freeing minks from their cages for a while, and start fighting specious specist terminology which exalts the human over other sentient beings. In the larger cause of altering the world's awareness of animals so that the part is not made greater than the whole, they should get "chairperson" changed to "chaircreature" and abolish phrases like "human dignity." Cat dignity, for instance, is far superior to the human variety, so why not just speak of dignity?

The much misapplied adjective *human* does seem to recognize animals, if only to exclude them. Why should the American Founding Fathers have talked about "human events," unless they feared that right around the corner from the Continental Congress were possum and bobcat and field-mouse events they would rather not deal with in their Declaration? There used to be a New York restaurant chain which advertised that its sandwiches were "untouched by human hands." What other hands cut off those crusts, I used to wonder: Raccoons'? Marmosets'?

In fact, people probably drag in the emotive word "human" to give weight, or merely rhythm, to some vapid statement like, "We must remove all barriers to human understanding." But lurking somewhere in the subconscious of these sentences may be a backhanded acknowledgment that animals are waiting in the wings.

154

For example, when the physicist Stephen Hawkings said, "The whole history of human thought has been to try to understand what the universe was like," was he admitting that cockroach thought may already have grasped it? When Jane Austen's Mr. Darcy speaks of "a circumstance [his sister's planned elopement] which no obligation should induce me to unfold to any human being," is he thinking of unfolding the dreadful secret to his English setter? And when Lord Hailsham, former Lord Chancellor of England, talked about "human litigation" in the House of Commons the other day, he may have wanted to make clear to the M.P.'s that he didn't mean a trial like the one in *Alice in Wonderland*, where the clerk of the court is a lizard.

Of course, the word *human* is sometimes used to distinguish us from machines, not animals. When the Russians put out feelers in 1983 for a "human contact meeting" with the Americans, they meant *human* as opposed to contact via telephone or air mail, not some wider animal contact between nations, with all that implies of cat or dog walks in the woods. And when a plane crashes because of "human error," one assumes the error they're ruling out is that of some computer, not a pilot fish.

But what's so great about "human values," compared to those of the seeing-eye dog? And then there are all those exclusively *human* things like necessity, tragedy, development, suffering, even life – to save a single one of which any amount of animal suffering is deemed OK. There's:

Human kindness (milk of)

Human spirit (triumph of against impossible odds)

Human element (we mustn't leave out the)

Human history (new era in, crime unparalleled in, etc; nary a footnote about lion, tiger or sea otter history)

Human consumption (unfit for. Chicken excrement is not considered unfit food for chickens, which are considered fit for. P.S. Ever taste Purina Cat Chow?)

Human enjoyment (ideas the highest form of, according to some mendacious academic I heard on the radio the other day)

Humanly possible ("I did everything that was." Nothing to what is porpoisely possible)

Human person ("a very warm and": a redundancy usually applied to some publicity-mad actor)

Human endeavor (nothing to elephant endeavor, or even chipmunk)

An especially lavish use of the word *human* comes from the pulpit, whence issued recently:

Human investigation (the miraculous as legitimate field of)

Human language (how impossible it is to explain the work of the Holy Spirit in, says British Bishop Trevor Huddleston. Has he tried pigeon English?)

Human race, The (God's masterpiece, according to bevies of pompous prelates. Oh, come off it! Go and contemplate a zebra!)

There are plenty of legitimate uses for this *H* word: Human chain, as distinct from the less effective daisy chain. The human condition, full of its special varieties of trouble, sorrow, need, sickness — and its propensity to bomb, torture, exploit and slander. Do we have to brag about it so much? Why can't we say with real, unaffected modesty: "I'm only human?"

Autumn Auction

HOST: *(For "All Things Considered")* The most important wine event in the world will take place this Sunday in Burgundy, in southeast France. It's a charity wine auction which has been held every year since medieval times to benefit an ancient hospital, or *hospice*, in the town of Beaune, the wine center of Burgundy. This auction sets the guidelines for the year's Burgundy prices, and wine merchants from New York to Tokyo flock to Beaune to attend the prestigious occasion and buy barrels of the latest vintage. Alice Furlaud is down in Beaune giving us a taste of things to come.

(Sound: the bells of the hospice of Beaune, rather like an ancient music box, are heard under my voice.)

ALICE: Beaune is a little town right out of *Puss in Boots*. And the bells of its great medieval hospice can be heard even out in the surrounding vineyards. The vines are bare now, and the new wine has just begun to age in cellars all over town. Down in the dark, vaulted cellar of the hospice it's nine o'clock in the morning, an ideal time for tasting. A solemn crowd of wine buyers are tasting wine from the great barrels that will be auctioned off on Sunday. *(Sounds of shuffling, murmuring, gargling and gossip.)* Wine merchant Jean-Pierre Nié was born upstairs in the hospice, and he's using his great-grandfather's silver *tastevin*, or wine-tasting cup, to decide between two different barrels of red Volnay Santenot. When describing wine, Jean-Pierre chooses his words with care.

JEAN-PIERRE NIÉ: Woody. It's a bit woody. It tastes a bit of the wood. This one is a delicate, feminine wine, I would say, and the other one would be a much more masculine wine with a lot of body: it's a heavy, good wine.

ALICE: Jean-Pierre is smelling it, breathing over it and making very strange faces. He's spitting on the floor . . .

JEAN-PIERRE NIÉ: *Pardon!* It has a very flowery nose. A good flowery nose. *(Sniff!)*

ALICE: *(Narrating) Nose,* in the world of wine, is another word for smell. It's one of those words that sound pretentious when people chat about bouquets and vintages and whirl wine around in their glasses just to show off. But here in Beaune, all the breathing and sniffing and gargling are authentic and practical. This is where all the wine terminology began, and these are the things you have to do to tell whether a cloudy, sour young Savigny-les-Beaune is going to grow up in a couple of years to be a great, velvety red wine.

At another tasting above ground in the Town Hall, I met Professor Paul Cadiau, an official taster of Beaune, who has a wine college. I asked him to show me exactly how it's done.

PAUL CADIAU: With my lips and my tongue I try to do like when we are drinking with a straw. I do this between my lips, my teeth — my former teeth — and my tongue, in order to expand all the wine inside of the mouth.

ALICE: OK, let's see you do it.

PAUL CADIAU: *(Gargling and swishing sound)* OK . . . Ah! My God!

ALICE: Professor Cadiau had tasted eighty-five wines already that day. To do this and keep your wits about you, you don't swallow the wine. You spit it on the floor — and at these crowded professional tastings I kept having to nimbly leap out of the way to avoid getting a mouthful all over my stockings. But in spite of all the spitting, wine tasting is heady work. Just to smell, as we did, about 20,000 bottles of Burgundy all open at once, is quite an experience — even for a professor of wine.

PAUL CADIAU: I'm not drunk at all, I'm quite normal! *(Sound of traffic as we weave down the street.)* I can tell you a few poems, if you want. Also singing! I'm drinking in the rain, I'm drinking a few drops! Not drops of rain but a few drops of wine — why not? Ha, ha, ha, ha. . . .

ALICE: *(Narrating)* Of course a lot of wine *is* actually being swallowed this week. The other night the Chevaliers du Tastevin, a famous brotherhood of wine freaks, gave a pre-auction dinner party for 580 people, in its own château, Clos de Vougeot. The château sits high on a hill among its vineyards, and the medieval rafters rang with drinking songs, while carefully choreographed waiters in regional costumes brought on course after course, each with its splendid wine. The theme for this dinner was the Statue of Liberty, and the guests of honor were American Ambassador to France Joe Rodgers and his wife, Honey.

(Fanfare of ancient hunting horns.)

JACQUES CHEVIGNARD: *(Head man of the order, wearing a musical-comedy medieval costume along with the rest of the top brass. There are times when it would be nice to have a camera along.)* Son Excellence Monsieur Joe Rodgers, Ambassadeur des Etats Unis d'Amérique! *(Enthusiastic applause and bravos.)*

ALICE: Mr. Rodgers was initiated into the order. They put a wine-tasting cup on a ribbon around his neck and gave him a huge silver goblet of wine to drink in one gulp. After the ceremony, he answered questions quite coherently.

AMBASSADOR RODGERS: Sure, I had to swear that I wouldn't drink anything but Burgundy wine for the rest of my life!

(Sound: the song "Chevaliers de la Table Ronde" sung in rollicking fashion by a huge hallful of distinguished imbibers. This fades and is replaced by sound of a peasanty band lurching along the street playing accordions and clarinets.)

ALICE: What with all this carousing in châteaux and the citizens of Beaune marching around the street waving plastic grapes, the soberest person in Beaune is probably the auctioneer, Monsieur Héry. He gave me a preview of his auction patter:

MONSIEUR HÉRY: Douze mille! Douze mille cinq cents! Allons bon, qui dit mieux? Treize mille!

ALICE: He'll have to go on like this for seven or eight hours on the day of the auction in the huge covered market. Only buyers are allowed inside, but crowds of people stand outside, eagerly listening to the bidding over loudspeakers. This is a town where the poorest inhabitants can give you precise figures on the proceeds of an auction in which only the very rich can participate. I've learned that last year the auction made 24,982,354 francs, or $13,831,649.39, for the hospice, and that the most expensive barrel was a red Corton

159

Vergennes which went for 116,000 francs a barrel. That's about twenty dollars a glass or four dollars a mouthful, and they're still talking about it. In an area where wine has been grown since 600 B.C., wine-consciousness goes deep—maybe back to the days of the Romans, when wine was a link to the gods. *(Sounds of auction: M. Hénry's running commentary, bids repeated, excited crowd sound.)* For National Public Radio, I'm Alice Furlaud, in Beaune, France.

OWL PROWL

HOST: (For "All Things Considered," Noah Adams in this case) Owl watching on the North Atlantic coast in January is one of the frostiest of winter activities. Alice Furlaud, who usually reports from France, where she says no one would go outdoors to look at any bird unless they were planning to eat it, is visiting on Cape Cod, Massachusetts. One cold night she joined seventeen hardy Cape Codders and an Audubon Society ranger to tramp around the woods in search of owls.

(Sound: a high, staccato whistle repeated many times. It keeps hooting and tooting through my narration.)

ALICE: That's the warning cry of a sawhet owl—or so the other owls in the forest are supposed to think. In actual fact, these hoots are not being uttered by a soft-feathered, nocturnal bird of prey, but by Peter Trull, a tall young ornithologist, leader of a late-night owl prowl through the White Cedar Swamp in Wellfleet, Massachusetts. The moon was full, and the temperature was around 20 degrees. We owl watchers were shivering in our down jackets, and the owls were probably shivering in their downy feathers. But Peter Trull was wearing only a sweater. Over the sounds of icy winds whooshing through the conifers and icy waves washing on the nearby ocean beach, Peter managed to teach us a lot about owls. For one thing, they don't just say "tu-wit tu-woo."

PETER TRULL: The other thing is that owls make all sorts of different sounds. You can hear an incredible cacophony of sounds that owls make, from twits to clucks to whistles to screams, literally. They even hiss a lot.

(Sound: cascading trills of notes, an owl call both musical and reflective.)

ALICE: Peter has a rare gift for all these owl languages, which he uses to "call in" the owls, as he puts it. The way to see owls, unlike daytime birds, is to get them to come and see *you*. If your hooting is good enough, they may mistake you for an owl in the dark, and hoot back. (*A higher trill, this time eerie.*) Then you can turn the flashlight on them.

That's the idea. But when an actual owl finally answered him, Peter seemed astonished.

PETER TRULL: (*In an awed and excited whisper*) Unbelievable! (*Whoo-whoo-whoo-whoo from owl.*) Gimme a flashlight, quick! Watch this, everybody. Are you all ready? *Sawhet owl!* Unbelievable! (*Moan of delight from a human being.*) Shh, shh! (*Real owl: whoo-whoo-whoo-whoo . . .*) Did you see that bird? (*Whoo-whooing of owl again.*) I want you all to know that's the first Sawhet owl I've ever called in! (*The little whistling hoot keeps on under my narration.*)

ALICE: The sawhet was a tiny owl, only five inches tall. He sat on a nearby branch peering at our group with great, round eyes. Then he faded from view like the Cheshire Cat. So we slogged on through the swamp in search of the heaviest owl in North America: the great horned owl.

The White Cedar Swamp is a scary place at night. It's a unique thirty-acre protected wetland, full of the almost-extinct White Atlantic Cedars. There are duckboards to walk on across the ice. (*Sound of boots on wooden ramp is heard here and there.*) And it's only about a mile from any number of Dunkin' Donuts, Captain Clambakes, and all the rest of the vacation development which is driving more and more owls into the swamp sanctuary. But when you fall behind the group on this walk, you think of those great horned owls hidden in the trees (*a low, definitely sinister whoo-whooing is heard throughout this speech*), with their five-foot wing spans and claws that seize and kill live prey. Owls eat mice, woodchucks, skunks—sometimes even black-and-white cats, which they mistake for skunks.

(*Sound: a strangled, squeaky scream.*)

ALICE: It was Peter's "small-mammal-in-distress cry," as he calls it, which attracted a great horned owl. (*Owl: Whoo! Whoo! Whoo-whoo-whoo.*)

PETER TRULL: Who did *not* hear the great horned owl? Raise your hand. (*Silence. Then a dramatic whisper:*) Hear it? I just called it now.

162

What you're hearing is a whoo-whoo-whoo, that's all. And it's real quiet.

ALICE: But Peter's triumph in owl-to-owl communication was a dialogue he had with a screech owl, who approached us for a good, long look—and then soared away across the moon.

PETER TRULL: *(gives a long, spine-chilling trill. Then another one.)* I want everybody to look for movement against the sky, because *(dramatic whisper)* there's a chance this bird will fly right in!
(Real owl: a liquid, bubbling trill.)
(Peter Trull: same trill, only louder.)
(Real owl: another string of notes, ending in woodpeckerlike taps.)
(Peter Trull: an imitation of the above which is perfect to the naked human ear.)
(Real owl: haunting trill as it flies away, growing fainter and fainter.)

ALICE: *(Narrating)* The Audubon Society encourages people to become fluent in Owl so that they can go out owling on their own, and become more conservation-minded. This plan may be a little hard on the owls, but it interests Jane Parker, an innkeeper from nearby Truro, just back from the owl prowl.

JANE PARKER: *(In a deep, husky voice)* You could get a tape of an owl. And then if you played that enough, and you learned to imitate that sound, you could go out by yourself and probably call in owls!

ALICE: Eventually the owls are going to catch on, and realize that half of the people, half of the owls in the woods have field glasses!

JANE PARKER: Yes, I kind of wondered if they didn't say, "Oh, for heaven's sakes!" as they flew away. I mean, you know!

ALICE: *(Narrating)* Peter Trull says the owls do catch on. No owl will ever have two conversations with him on the same evening.

PETER TRULL: There was no way I would have been able to get that screech owl to answer again. He observed humans, and said, "This isn't an owl. These are humans, and I'm leaving." And he left.

(The memory of the real owl's eerie trill runs through the rest of the piece.)

ALICE: *(Narrating)* As Christopher Robin said of his friend the Owl who lived in the Hundred Acre Wood, "Owl hasn't got brain exactly; but he knows things." *(Screech owl whistles wistfully for a while, then "All Things Considered" comes in with guitar over the whistling.)*

I'm proud of the recording I did for this feature. Peter Trull was afraid the lighted dials on my tape recorder would scare away the owls. So I had to hold my glove over the all-important needles that tell you at what sound level you're recording. I just moved the knob around to different positions in the dark, hoping at least one of the levels would be OK when an owl flew in. Manolli Weatherill, virtuoso sound engineer at NPR in New York, somehow managed to find the right kind of hoots on my cassettes and weave them together with fairy dust. We had such a mad time in the studio over this that we have been friends ever since.

Secrets Of The Pyramid 1989

This piece was broadcast on BBC's "Woman's Hour"; the introduction was read by Jenny Murray.

HOST: The new entrance to the Louvre—a sixty-six foot glass pyramid in the central courtyard designed by Chinese-American architect I. M. Pei, has been opened several times, with much fanfare, for selected visitors to see. But so far there hasn't *been* much to see. The other day France's minister of culture, Jack Lang, invited the foreign press to explore the great underground area beneath the pyramid, which is to add much-needed space to the Louvre. Alice Furlaud got an invitation to the evening reception.

ALICE: (*Narrating*) The purpose of the pyramid is to mark the entrance to the Louvre—soon to be revealed as an expanded, modern, Americanized museum. Actually, the Louvre was never meant to be a museum. For most of its life it was France's seat of government and the home of kings; and until last year there was still a government department within its walls. There has never *been* a main entrance to this immense collection of imposing buildings strung along the Seine. And it's been a sacred tradition *not* to be able to find the entrance to the museum. Here's the seventeen-year-old Miss Minnie Mortimer, my great-aunt-in-law, on her first visit to Paris with her parents and two little brothers on June 6, 1867.

MINNIE: (*Played by a demure-sounding Canadian girl of eighteen*) "Friday, Mama not being well, we could not do much of consequence. At twelve o'clock Richard, Stanley, Hattie Warren and myself started for the Louvre. We wandered around and around the courtyards but could not find the entrance to the picture gallery. So we had

165

to content ourselves with seeing a few pieces of statuary, which was very fine – although very old."

ALICE: And exactly eighty years later, also in June, also at the age of seventeen, I wrote in my diary:

"Went alone to the Louvre. Must have walked many miles trying to find the entrance to the museum; it turns out to be a small part of the whole thing. The Louvre is utterly divine, but you don't dare ask where the pictures are – there's a feeling of disapproval in the air. All I could find was acres of Egyptian tombs and statues."

ALICE: And forty years later, that same complaint was being heard from tourists of all nations.

AUSTRALIAN WOMAN: We finally, through word of fingers, and mannerisms, we got through, but then we couldn't find out how to get in *here!* So there's not good signs around. I think there should be more English signs as well as French and other nationalities; but apart from that, we love it.

ALICE: Surely a few well-placed signs would have been enough to guide the pilgrims to the *Mona Lisa?* Was it really necessary to put up a four-story high, 180-ton glass pyramid to show them the way into a new underground entrance in the middle of a courtyard? And *does* it show them the way in? The night of Minister Jack Lang's reception, guests found the front door of the pyramid roped off. We were told to go to the Rue de Rivoli façade of the Louvre and find some brand-new escalators which were supposed to lead us down into the base of the pyramid.

(Vox pop follows:)

WOMAN: How do you get in?

YOUNG MAN: You get in at the top there.

ALICE: Aha! Opposite the carousel?

WOMAN JOURNALIST: This is a way to get in, through here. This way!

PAT BRETT: No! That goes out to the street!

MAN: OK, we're looking for Mitterand's tomb. Because somewhere here he's – but they always keep that very concealed.

166

WOMAN JOURNALIST: Now if I walk up those stairs do you think I can get out?

ALICE: *(Narrating)* From inside, the pyramid is not the crystal-clear, transparent structure through which we expected to see the surrounding Louvre, but a kind of glass-covered erector set, a geometric creation of steel supports. And it's merely the roof of a deep central hall from which escalators fan out to the various galleries. There's also a Busby Berkeley-type staircase spiralling up into the air. This was closed off for our visit, but a Canadian television crew stepped over the rope and climbed up to explore the upper regions of the pyramid. They were never seen again, and their whitened bones may eventually be found, if the whole new Louvre is ever completely open to the public. But we'd been invited deep below to see the excavated remains of former royal strongholds, including the twelfth-century fortress built by Philippe Auguste, the first king of France to make the Louvre his castle.

We clumped along on duckboards through a beautiful labyrinth of honey-colored stone ramparts and columns and oubliettes—a strange contrast with the trendy airport-style architecture of the pyramid above. *(Over this, the clumping and clatter of a large group of journalists in the process of getting lost.)* It seemed ironic that in the process of deliberately transforming the Louvre from a palace with pictures into a pure-and-simple art museum, Mitterand's excavators discovered several other royal palaces on its site.

But we saw no signs of the boutiques, parking lots, diaper-changing rooms, movie theaters and restaurants under the pyramid which will make it possible to spend a day at the Louvre without seeing a single picture. Nor was there much evidence of the perfectly functioning I. M. Pei kind of museum which is planned—especially when most of the lights went out. *(Sound: babble of even-more-confused journalists.)* Not all the guests managed to grope their way in the dark to the buffet, where it was impossible to tell the miniature asparagus sandwiches from the miniature chocolate eclairs. But occasionally a bright light would flash on, hovering over the head of Minister of Culture Jack Lang, speaking to the press.

LANG: Our dream is to make a great modern museum, and for a long period the Louvre was not so well organized to welcome many people. My hope is that the visitors will be much more happy when they will come.

ALICE: Can you tell us how to get to the *Mona Lisa* from here?

LANG: Please?

ALICE AND PAT BRETT: The *Mona Lisa:* where do you find it from here?

LANG: It's in the same place!

ALICE: You're lost!

LANG: *(Beleaguered)* From here? Oh, yes, but how to explain to you through a microphone? No. When you will arrive in April here you will put the question at the entrance and immediately you will be — but I hope you will have the desire to discover also other paintings. . . . *(Fades down, protesting.)*

ALICE: *(Narrating)* If the pyramid is merely the tip of the iceberg in the "Grand Louvre," criticism of it has been very submerged. Rightwing people whisper that the Socialists wanted to complete the French Revolution of 200 years ago by planting an outrageous building inside the former seat of royal power. Another rumor hath it that the Freemasons are the bad guys, sneaking their symbol — a pyramid — into the historic heart of Paris. President Mitterand is a mason, some say, and he supposedly sits cross-legged in the pyramid at night, meditating on Isis and Osiris.

Saner dissenters wonder if the new underground Louvre is really worth the 200 million or so pounds it's costing to make the visitors, as Monsieur Lang says, "more happy." I'll leave the last word to tourist Minnie Mortimer, who finally managed to find the entrance on June 21, 1867:

MINNIE: "In the afternoon Mama and myself visited the Louvre. We had not much time to spend there, but had a general view of all the pictures. The generality of them were old and fading; not to my taste at all."

CANDIED VIOLETS: HOW VERY FRENCH

Crystallized violets is a subject that would seem to interest only turn-of-the-century women lying langorously in hammocks. Yet this story was dreamed up by the anything-but-langorous Margot Slade, editor of the New York Times Living *section, who has a genius for the esoterics of gastronomy.*

French people often eat violets, as anyone who has made a close study of French pastry can tell you. The little purple sugar flowers often seen on ornate cakes and candies in Paris patisserie windows are not a chef's imitation of violets but real violets that have been mummified in sugar. By themselves, these crystallized flowers, brittle and slightly perfumed, taste like bath salts. The flavor blends particularly well with chocolate. According to both a nineteenth-century confectioner's manual and the best-selling French herbalist, Maurice Mességue, candied violets are recommended for chest disorders.

The world's only manufacturer of *violettes cristallisées* is Dedieu Candi Flor, a small family company in the Toulouse suburb of Bonnefoy. Its specialty is known worldwide: the Queen of England may occasionally crunch a Dedieu violet, since Dedieu sells to her purveyor of chocolates, Charbonnel & Walker of Old Bond Street, London. Whether the Emperor of Japan has tried and enjoyed crystallized violets is unknown, but Japan is the company's newest and fastest-growing market.

Once the capital of the Visigoths, Toulouse has often been called the capital of violets—specifically, the luxurious, long-stemmed, double variety. Some Toulousains remember prewar days, when the Sunday market around the Romanesque church Saint Sernin, was purple with baskets of violets. Now, if anything, it is blue with blue jeans. Today, Toulouse is better known for its aviation and space industry. The Concorde was built here, and the first European space shuttle, *Hermès*, is expected to blast off from here in 1995.

But even now, with violets costing twenty-eight dollars for a bunch of fifty, there are reminders of the time when Toulouse was nicknamed "la cité de la violette." The city's football team wears violet shirts, and one can buy violet perfume, violet liqueur and, above all, the traditional violet-patterned miniature hat boxes of crystallized violets in every confectioner's and pastry shop in town for eleven dollars a pound.

Daniel Laffont, the forty-three-year-old owner of Dedieu Candi Flor, is candying violets as his father and uncle did before him, using mainly single violets from St.-Paul-de-Vence, near the Mediterranean coast. Ten employees in a big, shedlike room were hurriedly preserving the flowers in sugar with the companionable air of a family packing a last-minute picnic lunch. "It's necessary to put them very quickly in syrup to stop the aging of the flower—to keep this beauty as long as possible," Mr. Laffont says, pointing to a vat of violets floating in syrup that had turned purple. A worker scoops the flowers out with both hands, and another fluffs them gently in a dishpan until they harden just enough for dry sugar to stick but not caramelize.

The violets go next into a small tumbler that turns them slowly as pale mauve sugar is added. The mauve coloring is American, as Food and Drug Administration regulations require if they are to be sold in the United States.

After the tumbling, excess sugar is manually removed, and Dedieu Candi Flor's brand-new assembly-line technology takes over. The violets go on conveyor belts through a drying machine designed by Mr. Laffont and an engineer friend that shortens the drying process to one day—it used to take two or three days. Once dry, the flowers are surprisingly tough, and workers scrape them off trays as roughly and noisily as barnacles off a boat.

Mr. Laffont's company candies thirty-five tons of flowers a year, ten tons of which are violets. The rest are roses, mimosa, holly, lilacs and mint leaves that are sold wholesale for cake and candy decoration. Half the flowers are exported.

Despite expansion in the twelve years since he took over, Mr. Laffont says the comestible violet business has fallen from its heyday before the war, when Dedieu shared the industry with four or five other local concerns. The Marquise de Chabannes La Palice recalls a surplus of violets in Toulouse in June 1940, when she arrived on foot among crowds of Parisians fleeing from German troops. "There wasn't a thing to eat in the entire town but crystallized violets. The refugees had been through it like locusts and they'd eaten every crumb of bread, and the shop windows had nothing in them at all but those little round boxes of violets. I can tell you, when you're sleeping in a church pew and you're ravenous, candied violets are very insufficient."

No one knows who cast the first violet in solid sugar; probably not the Visigoths. Candied violets seem to have made their first appearance in the 1860s, when Toulouse first cultivated them commercially. In those days, most were grown in Lalande, a northern suburb. The maraichères bearing baskets of violets on their heads and wearing long, striped skirts walked their flowers to market.

Today, retired maraichères mourn the past. "It's finished, finished. And yet it was a pretty métier!" exclaims Blanche Albus, as she looks out her window over acres of derelict brick foundations that once supported greenhouse frames. At eighty-five, Mrs. Albus, who blames industrialization and the highway for the end of the violet era, says: "Young people won't do all that stooping to thin out the violets and pick them. In our greenhouse, we only have two rows left, just enough for my daughter to sell at the cemetery on Sundays."

Henri Berdoues, a manufacturer of violet perfume, says, "Fifty years ago, we used to buy ten tons of violet leaves every year here in Toulouse. Last year, we could only find one ton." Most of Mr. Berdoues's violets come from Grasse in the south, which is also a source for Georges Serres, a maker of violet liqueur. Mr. Serres, who is planning an American sales campaign, has put together what he calls an explosive cocktail composed of his liqueur, vodka, champagne and pear liqueur. It is topped with crèmè fraîche and sprinkled with crystallized violets. Both Mr. Serres and Mr. Berdoues, patriarchs of old family businesses employing ten to twelve people, need only a token number of Toulouse violets to keep the name "Toulouse" on their product labels.

But Mr. Laffont wants as many native violets as possible to maintain the traditional look of his product. He has his eye on a possible solution, cloning violets in test tubes.

OLD PALS COME TO PARIS

In late spring and early summer, we American residents of Paris become very popular with vacationing American friends from our hometowns. They show up in droves, expecting us to provide beds and stop whatever we're doing and introduce them to La Vie Parisienne. On behalf of all my fellow expatriates who suffer from living in a prime tourist site, I wrote this commentary for "All Things Considered."

ALICE: They start arriving in early June, and at first it's kind of fun having the living room of my two-room Paris apartment carpeted with college students. But it's hard to work when you're interrupted every few minutes with questions, endless questions: "How do I get to the Musée d'Orsay on the Metro?" "Can we drink the water?" "What's the French for high-speed Fujichrome?"

But just now I got a letter from a middle-aged friend who's much too elegant to want to sleep on my floor. It's on thick, creamy office stationery and dictated to a secretary with the initials "jg." It starts: "Hooray! We're coming to Paris on September 25th for one night!" That's nice. Next he says, "We'll have the baby in tow, so you'll get to meet him." Hm. First I've heard of a baby, but anything could have happened in the two years or so since I've heard from my friend. Next the letter explains that he and his new young wife and baby will be in Paris on their way down to Agen in southwest France, where an American movie-star friend has lent them a château for two weeks. Clearly these people move in top circles, and they want me to have dinner with them that first night in Paris. Hooray! And the next morning, the letter says, they want me to go down to this château with them for a couple of days. Hooray, hooray! But wait!

The letter says he wants me to find them a hotel for that one night in Paris, near a park. Now there are very *few* parks in Paris. Could my friend have confused Paris with London? Anyway he says he wants a suite with a crib for the baby, and furthermore it's *vital* (his italics, not mine) that this hotel room be ready by 9:00 A.M. He wants me to make a reservation for dinner in a quiet restaurant with one or two stars not far from the hotel, and not later than eight o'clock. He wants me to arrange for a babysitter while we're having dinner. Then, for the trip to the château, he wants me to get train tickets to Agen, in a first-class compartment.

I'm beginning to wonder if these "couple of days" I've been invited for will be enough to recover from an eight-hour train ride with a baby under two, even in a first-class compartment — if such a thing exists outside of a Hitchcock movie. And wait, there's a P.S. A rented car must meet the train, "medium-sized but with four doors and a baby seat." That kind of car is going to be about as easy to obtain in the French provinces as a pumpkin coach drawn by eight mice! And the letter ends, "P.P.S.: Be sure the hotel has a stroller."

Now this invitation is beginning to look too much like work. Hooray, hooray, nothing. I'm sending an answer, typewritten by a fictitious secretary, initials "ng." It says, "Alice Furlaud is out of the country for an indefinite time and her mail is not being forwarded. P.S. She does not know the French word for stroller."

MARINA REVISITED

Every summer, free-lance journalists rush around the Eastern Seaboard of the United States, trying to combine their nonpaid vacations with stories about loon-calling contests, Blueberry Pancake Breakfasts and old-car rallies. I spend my summers in Maine, but in such primitive conditions that free-lancing is a real challenge. My mother's cabin has no telephone or electricity and her car is on the borderline of automobile blight, much aggravated by the long dirt road to the village. Telephoning a story to the New York Times from the boothless telephone on the grocery store porch can be embarrassing. Describing some neighbor who makes teddy bears out of old coats for the Methodist church bazaar, I'll be about to shout down the telephone to the New York Times copy-taking machine: "Mrs. Hatch, seventy-six . . . ," when Mrs. Hatch stumps up the grocery porch steps and I have to hastily lower my voice to a whisper.

For radio work, the nearest recording studio is forty-five minutes away and owned by a Christian group who kindly charge NPR practically nothing for exhausting producing sessions. If under pressure I shriek "dammit!" or something, I don't dare glance at Stu, the adorable sound engineer, for fear he may be turning pale. But I record simple commentaries myself in the cabin late at night, when the motorboats have all gone to bed.

HOST: Alice Furlaud has spent the past thirty summers living primitively on a lonely stretch of the Maine coast. This year she arrived at her one-room cabin to find that a large house was being built 150 feet away. From the waterside, she sends us this lament:

(Sound: *lapping waters of Penobscot Bay over following script:*)

ALICE: Until this summer, the only houses you could see from here were a few old cottages and a lighthouse on the island across the bay. This is the coast T. S. Eliot must have meant in his poem "Marina," all about grey rocks and scent of pine and the wood thrush singing through the fog. And now there's a cruel yellow gash in that dark green fringe of fir trees behind the grey rocks, and every morning at eight—a time when I'm having breakfast out here on a stump— the squeal of buzz saws and the thud of hammers float across the water. Usually I have a bath out here, in an old tin tub with water from the rain barrel. This ritual will have to go, now that it can be seen from several big windows and from that terrace that's been bulldozed out of the fir tree roots. The same goes for swimming off these rocks with no bathing suit on. And my daily forest walk to the squeaky old well where I draw the drinking water has lost its magic. There's always been a mysterious, Red Riding Hood atmosphere around this well, and now just across the dirt road from it, there's the big, brightly shingled façade of this house, with its multilevel roofs and its edges bound in shiny metal: a house meant for a suburb, and a house that will soon be crying out for a telephone—something so far unknown in this fragile paradise.

I keep trying to ease the pain of this invasion, this new presence that's there wounding every quiet morning. I read uplifting books that tell me how a healthy mind adapts to change. Ben Jonson tells me how "in short measures life may perfect be." But they are such short measures: pauses between bouts of electric drilling; the builders' lunch hour. I tell myself that no one owning a mere half acre has the right to expect the landscape all around them to stay the same, that owning a half an acre anywhere is a rare privilege in a world full of homeless people. I tell myself the house will weather and merge more with the trees. But I know that civilization will be that much nearer this dreamy seascape, and that after the hammering will come the time, as Eliot says, when "human voices wake us, and we drown."

Just now I turned my back on the new house and distributed pieces of baked potato to some swooping seagulls. How did their ancestors feel when my family built this cabin? And who knows what a shock it was to the local seagulls, and red squirrels, and chipmunks, and that wood thrush calling through the fog?

For National Public Radio, I'm Alice Furlaud, on the Penobscot Bay in Maine.

LA LÉGION D'AMOUR

HOST: Paris is often called the world's most romantic city—partly because of the exceptionally large number of lovers embracing and kissing in public—everywhere from café tables to the middle of the Champs Elysées. It may shock tourists to learn that roughly one-third of these outdoor lovers are employees of the French government, paid to behave amorously on the streets to boost Paris's image as the City of Love. A small government department with the acronym COMSI is devoted to this work, headed by an eighty-year-old ex-paratrooper called Colonel Auguste Viollet-le-Duc Bèze. Our reporter Alice Furlaud went on an inspection tour of Colonel Bèze's amatory troops—starting with a visit to the COMSI offices in one of the towers of the Palais de Justice. She asked the colonel what the initials COMSI stand for.

LE COLONEL: *(With command center sounds in background)* You must realize that in France all organizations have initials, and this means the Organization for the Metropolitan Preservation of Intimate Sentimentality . . . *(translates briskly)* . . . Caisse d'Organization Metropolitaine de la Sentimentalité Intime.

ALICE: How did COMSI actually get started?

LE COLONEL: Well, it started in May 1968 at the desire of Général de Gaulle, who was deeply concerned by the lack of public affection in the streets of Paris. For centuries the thing which has given Paris its special quality has been the lovers in the cafés, in the parks, on the quais and so forth and so on, and these people were beginning to stay home too much, interested in television, interested in politics and so on, and we wanted to put love out on the streets.

ALICE: But surely if these people are hired by the government and paid to go and kiss on park benches it's not really a spontaneous— what I mean is you're not giving a true picture.

LE COLONEL: What is play and what is work is another question altogether. Now if you'll excuse me I see something on the map! *(Calls to subordinates:)* Qu'est-ce-qu'il y a à Chatou?

ALICE: Now one whole wall of this room is a map of Paris. *(To le Colonel:)* Could you explain what . . . Oh, sorry. He's making a telephone call.

LE COLONEL: I'm a little concerned because there is no . . . *(into telephone:)* Qu'est-ce que vous avez á Chatou? Alors il n'y a personne á Chatou, dépêchez-vous, vite! *(Slams down telephone.)*

ALICE: Could you explain to us what that was all about? Now you have this map on the wall with pins stuck in strategic places.

LE COLONEL: Yes, the pins indicate the troops. I was having a telephone with the supervisors. We have a number of supervisors who visit all the locations where the troops are supposed to be—and it was reported if you notice this gap here, you see, Chatou is the island in the Seine where they have the Ham and Junk Fair there at the moment, and it's very important and there's no one there!

ALICE: Colonel Bèze, our information is that your budget, your yearly budget for COMSI, is 408 million francs a year—that's about 68 million dollars. Is that a correct figure?

LE COLONEL: The question of budget is closed for consideration publicly, you see, but I can tell you that there is one project which Président Mitterand and Prime Minister Chirac are in complete agreement about, and that is the COMSI program. They have never subtracted one centime from the budget and they on the *contraire* have added every year. Now! Shall we get up and I think go out and review troops in action. *(Hums "Marseillaise.")*

(Bells of Notre Dame with Alice and le Colonel out of doors.)

ALICE: So, Colonel Bèze and I are sitting on a bench in a park behind the east end of Notre Dame. It's one of the first sunny days of spring, and there are purple pansies in the central garden.

177

LE COLONEL: It's charming, most charming.

ALICE: It is lovely, isn't it, and there are benches—many, many benches with many, many people on them.

LE COLONEL: You're not lacking in charm yourself, if I may say so.

ALICE: Oh no, no no, no. *(I pull myself together.)* Well, the benches are awfully full. There are children, old ladies, and quite a lot of couples, but I mean they're real couples, aren't they?

LE COLONEL: Well, I don't know exactly what you mean by real couples. But some of them are our people, of course!

ALICE: Not really!

LE COLONEL: The young man, they're doing very nicely . . . the young man with the Mickey Mouse sweater.

ALICE: And the girl. Oh my heavens! They are really hired by your department?

LE COLONEL: They're apprentices, actually. In fact I have to make a note of this, I think he's going a bit too far. Come along with me. I would like to show you . . . Don't point. Let's look this way because it's preferable.

ALICE: Now he's looking at a couple, both in denim jackets, completely involved in a very deep and long kiss. Well, I think they're acting too well, Colonel Bèze: are those really your troops?

LE COLONEL: They certainly are. They certainly are. And it's *such* a pleasure for me.

ALICE: I won't point, but what about those two?

LE COLONEL: They're amateurs!

ALICE: Oh, you know all yours by sight?

LE COLONEL: Of course. Not only by sight. I know them very deeply, personally.

ALICE: Do you yourself train your loving couples?

LE COLONEL: Well, up to now I have trained them all personally myself. In the last few years I have tried to develop some assistants who will carry the work on without me, so that when I am called back from my internal exile, so to speak, in this world, the work will go on. It is work that is not like work. It is work that is like wisdom.

LIBERTÉ, EGALITÉ, TRAFFIC

"La Légion d'Amour" is my radio version of a story Max wrote in
Metro *magazine, a kind of predecessor to Paris Passion. It caused something of a sensation, with the photographic agency Magnum calling
the paper to get Colonel Bèze's telephone number so they could photograph him, and quite a few other inquiries. In my version Max played
Colonel Bèze, ad-libbing the lines as usual. The Colonel has become
quite real to both of us: when we see couples kissing on benches in
the Tuileries or in the library at the Pompidou Center, our first
thought is usually "Colonel Bèze's troops on duty!"*

*But if Colonel Bèze had been a real French official, I would never
have been persistent enough to actually get an interview with him.
Trying to persuade press secretaries of important people in France
can easily involve several weeks of telephoned and written requests
which are very often refused—at least at first. I have never had a knack
for famous people, anyway. When they see me coming they generally crouch behind a hedge or hide their heads in paper bags. Never
could I be one of those enviable journalists who write in their memoirs,
"The general secretary's staff had warned me that he could only give
me a five-minute interview. So both of us were surprised when we
glanced up at Catherine the Great's ormulu clock and realized we had
been talking for an hour and a half."*

*But on being assigned a story about the tottering Arc de Triomphe,
I did go to see former President Valéry Giscard d'Estaing, a privilege
which I attribute to his having that great rarity in France: a pleasant,
intelligent, unobstructive—even helpful!—secretary. The interview
was in his house, where the surroundings were so opulent I wanted
to lie down and roll in them. Before I could do so, in came the great
man himself in a V-neck Abercrombie & Fitch sweater. His*

gentleman-of-the-old-school demeanor made me feel like the foreign-correspondent-of-the-old-school, and all went well.

The "All Things Considered" host, Renée Montagne, with whom I've had some lovely times capering around Paris, started my Arc de Triomphe piece thus:

HOST: The Arc de Triomphe is as much a symbol of France as the Eiffel Tower, but right now it's not half as steady. The Arc, which was begun in Napoleon's time to commemorate his victories, is beginning to totter. As a result, cracks are appearing in the façade, and so many pieces of sculpture have been falling off it that they recently put up a safety net. A nationwide fund-raising campaign has just been launched to shore up the giant monument. Alice Furlaud braved the motorcar stampede up at the Etoile the other day, just to be sure the Arc was still there.

(Sound: a police whistle amidst the whoosh and squeal and rush of traffic at the Etoile in Paris. This is heard under my narration.)

ALICE: The most lethal traffic in the world swarms around and around the Arc de Triomphe, and it's a wonder it hasn't killed the monument before now with vibrations and exhaust fumes. But it seems it's not the traffic but the rain, seeping year after year into the base of the arch, which has been causing pieces of sculpture to fall among the tourists. Or so says Monsieur Michel Marot, Architect-in-Chief of the Buildings and Palaces of France, with special responsibility for maintaining the Arc de Triomphe. I talked to him on the very top of it.

MONSIEUR MAROT: It is only the foundation. Between the stones there is a joint and these joints are weak. The weakness of the joints come from the rain, which is washing sands and cement, and when you press on the sands it is going on down.

ALICE: You mean it's crumbling from underneath?

MONSIEUR MAROT: Yes.

ALICE: But why would that make the stones fall? Let's see, we're right on top of it now. . . .

MONSIEUR MAROT: When the building is going down, the cracks are on the sculpture.

181

ALICE: *(Narrating)* Sand is the theme which has been taken up by the fund-raising committee to save the arch. The other day they launched on the television airwaves an appeal which shows the Arc de Triomphe as a sand castle dissolving in the wind.

(Sound: whistling wind and lonely desert sound from TV ad, with broadcaster's appeal beginning, "Le temps menace l'Arc de Triomphe," fades under my narration.)

ALICE: The initiative to rescue the Arc de Triomphe came, oddly enough, from American Express, the credit card people. But the French themselves soon got into the act, and the former President of France, Valéry Giscard d'Estaing, is now president of the Association for the Restoration of the Arc de Triomphe. Monsieur Giscard d'Estaing has laid more wreaths at the Tomb of the Unknown Soldier than he can count. He can describe Napoleon's funeral at the Arc as if he'd been there; and also the parade, or *défilé*, of the victorious Allies, after World War I.

GISCARD: There are pictures of the *défilé* of 1919, with the famous American generals on their horses. The French horses were white and I suppose the American horses were brown.

ALICE: Sort of like a western movie?

GISCARD: Yes! Ha, ha, ha, ha. . . .

ALICE: *(Narrating)* Even when the Paris traffic, or *circulation*, consisted of horses, it still swirled madly around the site of the Arc de Triomphe, according to Monsieur Giscard d'Estaing. The great meeting point of twelve avenues is called the Etoile, or star, because the high ground on which the Arc de Triomphe now stands was originally a meeting point of bridle paths.

GISCARD: There was a forest there until the seventeenth century, and it was just in the wood, an *étoile* of roads, a crossing of roads. So it's quite in the center of all the neighboring avenues, and to entirely eliminate the circulation would be almost impossible. But sometimes by chance you have the opportunity of seeing it empty. I did as the president, because when you go for a ceremony it is empty. And also very early in the morning, sometimes at sunrise you can see it, and of course it's much more beautiful.

(Sounds of footsteps on stone, doors clanging, voices on various levels of the Arc, heard under the following:)

ALICE: *(Narrating)* Michel Marot can see the Arc de Triomphe empty any time he wants to. He's the absolute monarch of the Arc, and he's the only man in France who's allowed to leave his car right outside the Arc with its motor running, while everyone else has to walk in from underground. To follow Monsieur Marot around the Arc de Triomphe with uniformed guards rushing ahead to unlock secret doors for him, is quite a trip. It was Monsieur Marot who festooned the great grey safety net, like a veil on an old lady's hat. He's already making drawings for a huge temporary sculpture to put on top of the Arc de Triomphe for the 200th anniversary of the French Revolution next year. And it's Monsieur Marot who has worked out a plan to keep the Arc de Triomphe from falling into the Metro.

MONSIEUR MAROT: We are going to put armature—how do you say armature?

ALICE: I think you say armature, at least you do with sculpture.

MONSIEUR MAROT: Armature—above the vaults inside the building to keep it—not moving. And we have to *injecter*—?

ALICE: To inject.

MONSIEUR MAROT: To inject cement inside the joints of the foundation.

ALICE: You're going to give it injections of cement? That's going to be interesting!

MONSIEUR MAROT: We have to keep the rain away of the esplanade, that's all.

ALICE: Do you mean the traffic did *not* have a bad effect on the Arc de Triomphe?

MONSIEUR MAROT: Not at all.

(Sound: frantic traffic around the Etoile heard under narration.)

ALICE: I don't believe him. I think the Arc de Triomphe is being shaken to pieces by too many internal combustion engines. And I suspect that to Monsieur Marot and Monsieur Giscard d'Estaing, Paris traffic is as sacred an institution as the Arc de Triomphe itself. To zoom aggressively around the Etoile is the inalienable right of all French citizens, just like Liberté, Egalité and Fraternité. But how would the Emperor Napoleon, who dreamed up this 50,000-ton edifice to glorify himself, have felt about it? Would he really have wanted his majestic triumphal arch to be the center of a whizzing whirlpool of Renaults and Peugeots and Citroens, all driving to maim? I hate to tell you, but I think he would have *just loved it*. For National Public Radio, I'm Alice Furlaud, in Paris.

The "Marseillaise"—a rousing, brassy version by the Garde Republi- caine band, comes crashing in here, mixed with the mad Etoile traf- fic, recorded by me and my friend Linda White at the risk of our lives. Along with the angry whizzing of the automobiles, we got the hee- haw of an occasional fire truck, the higher and more nervous bray of an ambulance, and highest-pitched and most hysterical of all—the ululations of the police vans. NPR's Karen Breslau, a real artist at such things, mixed the piece and made me a special long version of this melange of the sounds of Paris, lasting till the very end of the national anthem. If some day I have to leave Paris forever, this min- ute or so of "ambience" will bring back to me in a rush all the absurd contrasts, the great scenic sweeps, the sound and fury and funniness and just plain glory of living in France.

APOLOGIA PRO CAREERA SUA

By now the reader (or skimmer) will have realized that my short journalistic life has not been an exciting one. I have not smuggled my tape recorder into a Tibetan monk's cave, or been led blindfolded on muleback to the mountain hideouts of any guerrilla leaders (actually, now I think of it, I am negotiating to meet some radical animal rights people who may well require a blindfold). Although only a few of my radio scripts are in this book, you could call it "Chronicle of a Wasted Life."

I'm always amazed at all these people I read about who "have no regrets." I don't think I've heard a single celebrity from Boy George to George Bush admit they have a single regret. Is that why they succeeded? Perhaps. Regrets are bad for you, body and mind. But I regret everything. Everything!

I regret that I didn't learn to skate well enough at age ten or so to do outside loops at Mrs. Marshall's skating parties in Baltimore. I regret that I didn't follow the advice of Thornton Wilder, who oversaw the Harvard Dramatic Club's production of his play *Skin of Our Teeth*, which ran for two whole weeks, and in which I had the more-or-less leading role of Sabina, the maid. Mr. Wilder, over coffee at the late lamented St. Clair's tearoom, asked me to "Promise me you will play my Emily."

I had found *Our Town* in a bookshelf at home when I was nine, and Emily's line, "Mother, please look at me!" had haunted me ever since. But the only line I ever spoke on the professional stage was, "I shall be the soup!" in a Brattle Theater production of *Androcles and the Lion*—my father called it "Androcles and the line." Right after that I got married and went to sleep for a hundred years.

I regret that I didn't have a tape recorder during the year and a half my husband and I spent as domestic servants in California, or when we worked in a needlepoint-kit factory in London, where the wisecracks from our fellow wool sorters were right out of Monty Python. And I could have recorded some lovely actualities when I was a Christmas-season salesgirl in the gift department of Bonwit Teller's in New York (especially the dreaded early-morning pep talks by the floor walkers about objects upon which no one could rest their eyes with pleasure for two seconds: "This cachepot has a Meissen motif and a Swiss music box in the base which plays 'Tit Willow.' Push it, girls! Push it!").

I wish I could have recorded some of the sounds of a three-week trip to the Soviet Union—where we were taken by two madly generous friends—beginning in Armenia, which even then had a grim, harsh sadness in its very countryside. But those were the days when your Intourist guide took you behind a tree and whispered, "Do you know the words to 'Jesus Christ Superstar'?"

I regret that I didn't record the Swiss Federal Yodelling Contest, attended by participants in their cantonal costumes from all over Switzerland, some with bell-like and others with hound-dog voices. We went with our Indian guru, U. G. Krishnamurti. When my husband said, "This is what the angels sound like!" U. G. asked, with surprising humility, "Do you really think so? Do the angels sound like this?"

I regret that I never recorded the wild, wicked, purely joyful laugh of my friend Nancy Newbold Brien, a sound I used to miss very often, even before she died, unbelievably, last year. I regret that I recorded only a few fragments of my father's voice.

I wish I could have taped my dash with Penelope Hughes down the flooded River Rhone on a Zodiac rubber raft in, of all months, May 1968. But we were either holding on tight, steering just barely clear of the whirlpools which kept trying to engulf us underneath every bridge, or fending off the bulls and mosquitoes of the Camargue, as well as late-night shad fishermen trying to invade our sleeping bags. (Penny and I began at about age five to form our own special and hopeless criteria by which to judge the world around us. We assumed, wrongly, that all civilized people wanted to protect the unselfconscious landscapes we loved, full of peeling old houses that no one thought of as "landmarks" or "antiques"; scummy, green, forgotten ponds; and overgrown bridle paths and trolley tracks that went nowhere.)

My first summer in France, at the age of seventeen, when I boarded with a teacher in a primitive cottage on the coast of Brittany and went out fishing with boatloads of rugged Bretons who spoke no French, happened before cassette recorders or National Public Radio existed. To regret not getting those strange voices on tape would be like regretting that no one tape-recorded the Battle of Antietam. But it's this kind of memory which often saves me from out-and-out envy of my young fellow reporters who go swashbuckling around Paris carrying their brand-new recording equipment, with ministers of state trying to seduce them right and left:* they never knew France when it was a foreign country. They didn't know the literally breathtaking excitement of getting off an ocean liner into a scene full of blue-smocked porters yelping at each other, in which every detail of life was different—except an occasional bar of Palmolive soap, which stood out, in 1947, as the only American product in all of France.

My reporter pals didn't come over to live in the Real France: They came to live in the familiar, homey environment of MacDonald's and Madonna and Mr. Clean and Coca Cola and chocolate-chip cookies and Benetton and Toshiba and, most universal of all, blue jeans. When I first came to France I brought a denim skirt my mother made. (My mother invented the denim skirt: about this there is absolutely no question. Ask anybody.) French people turned around to stare at me in the street when I wore this skirt. Americans looked as odd to the French then as the French, with their little string gloves, looked to us. They would ask us if we "knew any Red Indians" (*peaux rouges*). Young expatriates of today never experienced third class on a French train with wooden slat seats and live chickens among the luggage. They didn't know the France where elegant women wore nothing, ever, but black on the street, and where if you asked to use the bathroom you were never asked back. Luckily, my young American woman friends are too sophisticated to recoil with horror, as we did, at the sight of Frenchmen in their jock-strappish

---

* I feel it only fair to myself to report here that even I, at my present age fifty-eight, was the object of a manfully determined pursuit by a very distinguished Frenchman around a very distinguished national monument somewhere in France—on Christmas Eve.

bathing suits. And their mothers certainly didn't send them over here as mine did, with the admonition, "Remember, you are an ambassador for your country!" By this she meant that I would be in places where no one had ever seen an American, so it was important that I make a good impression. Find such a place in France today and I'll give you a thousand francs!

I hope I was an acceptable ambassador for my country in the tiny village of Albiez-le-Vieux in the Savoie Mountains, where I went to ski in 1949 with a group of students, all of them French but me. None of the villagers had ever seen a Parisian, much less an American. We stayed in a youth hostel which we found, after a two-day train and bus trip down there, to be unfinished, with no plumbing or running water, and worse, no glass in the windows. As for the people of the village, you would have to go to the Middle East now to find lives as hard as theirs. I remember their wooden faces with lines like bark, and very few teeth. They were, however, warmer than we were: they lived in their barns – or the cows lived in the living room, whichever way you like to think of it – and this provided central heating. The only family living room that had no cows in it was known as "the café." The woman of the house brought out drinks and coffee from the kitchen; her babies crawled on the floor, and there all day sat the curé, gently stewing in glass after glass of wine. Cooking was done in the public baking oven, where on Christmas Eve we students roasted the turkey we had travelled miles on a bus to procure. The medical student used a syringe to inject this fowl with brandy at intervals between walking up the mountain and skiing back down. At midnight mass, the congregation sang the "Cantique de Noël." That's one sound my young colleagues are unlikely to have recorded: Christmas music sung by people who have never heard any singing but their own.

Everything else, though, I envy them terribly. I know it's supposed to hearten women of my age these days, that all the women's pages are praising the "homely, unvarnished style" of Barbara Bush. Mrs. Bush "has become America's newest fashion idol," says the *London Sunday Times*, which claims that American fashion magazines are full of "mature models with greying hair and sensible clothing." I must say I haven't noticed any signs of this new fashion on the Paris streets. And actually, how unvarnished *is* Mrs. Bush? In her purse she carries only "the basics" of make-up, says one magazine: a folding hairbrush, lipstick, and "blusher." I don't know what "blusher" is exactly: it sounds like some sort of yuppie version of rouge. If Mrs. Bush were the real old bag of the 1940s they all say she is, she'd just rub some lipstick on her cheeks when necessary, the way the rest of us do.

The fact is that in my case make-up doesn't seem to help. Once, staying in a grand palace in a southern French town, I did spend quite a while putting on mascara and Max Factor liquid powder and white eyelids and God knows what else, to impress my dazzling jet-set psychologist host. That evening he took my face in both his hands and mused, "I wonder what you'd look like with make-up on." But being less varnished than even Barbara does not mean I am happy with my own careworn look, even if it is the latest style. I hate every single thing about "aging." I can't tell you the rosebuds I wish I'd gathered, and when I think of how I used to flounce affrontedly past all those men of yore who were kind enough to whistle at me in the streets, my gosh, I'd like to go back there and shake all their hands and thank them, the old sexist monsters.

Luckily the reporter is invisible on the radio. But anyway I've got too many plans to go around mourning for my lost youth! I'd like to do some good with my tape recorder. I'd love to move and shake a few events as my old friend Anne Wyman of the *Boston Globe* did, with a series of articles on a family with a Downs Syndrome child, who were resisting sending her to an institution. Because of Anne's stories, there is a unique section of Massachusetts law which allows Medicaid to pay for home care for such children. And wouldn't I love to be in the shoes of Jenny Devitt, a Paris-based radio journalist who is writing an hour-long documentary on the bear population of Europe—even if it is for television. I would love to help save some endangered creature such as the Jentink's Duiker, an antelope which lives in the dwindling forests of the Ivory Coast. While there I could find out if it's really true, as a Ghanaian once told me, that the people on the streets of Abijan are just as snappish and unfriendly as the Parisians.

I may try to investigate the murky depths of France's intellectual world, storm the Académie Francaise and see why its members need spinach-green uniforms and swords for the task of creating a dictionary. And I'd like to find out what the French Foreign Legion is up to these days—joining under an assumed name. Because even for recording a trek across the desert to Sidi al Abbès—if it's still there—I submit that radio is a better medium than television. Radio lets you keep your own soul and your own judgment: it lets you form your own images. But with TV swamping us from one side and radio music washing over us from the other, the radio documentary may be as threatened a species as the Jentink's Duiker.

My mother dragoons her Massachusetts neighbors into listening to me by simply standing over them till the broadcast is over. The only feedback I've ever received from all but one of these victims came when I appeared briefly on the "NBC Nightly News," being interviewed one freezing night during a Paris electricity strike. I sounded stupid and looked foul in my husband's overcoat worn over two flannel nightgowns, smashing orange crates to burn in the fireplace. I hadn't really expected this camera crew, complete with tons of equipment and a natty correspondent who had to sit on the bed. And my appearance blew the image I'd been trying to convey when in the U.S., of my life in Paris discussing *ideés générales* in a damask-hung salon. But on my next visit home, my mother's friends positively flocked to say, with a certain respect, "I saw you on *television!*"

It all makes me feel like Peter Pan standing out on the stage, begging the pantomime audience to save Tinkerbell's life: "If you believe in fairies, clap your hands!" I'd like to say to all listeners—the captive ones listening in their cars, the potential ones who prefer the less skillful, more wasteful and much more expensive medium of television: If you believe your ears, unplug your Walkman and your computer and even your TV for a few minutes. Save the fragile and fleeting radio feature!